THE
LITURGY
The Source and Summit of Our Christian Life

Corinna Laughlin

LTP
LITURGY
TRAINING
PUBLICATIONS

Nihil Obstat
Reverend Mister Daniel G. Welter, JD
Chancellor
Archdiocese of Chicago
January 24, 2018

Imprimatur
Very Reverend Ronald A. Hicks
Vicar General
Archdiocese of Chicago
January 24, 2018

The *Nihil Obstat* and *Imprimatur* are declarations that the material is free from doctrinal or moral error, and thus is granted permission to publish in accordance with c. 827. No legal responsibility is assumed by the grant of this permission. No implication is contained herein that those who have granted the *Nihil Obstat* and *Imprimatur* agree with the content, opinions, or statements expressed.

This book was edited by Danielle A. Noe, MDIV. Christian Rocha was the production editor and Kari Nicholls was the designer and production artist.

Source and Summit painting by Lalo Garcia, commissioned in 2013 by Liturgy Training Publications.

22 21 20 19 18   1 2 3 4 5

Printed in the United States of America

Library of Congress Control Number: 2018938614

ISBN 978-1-61671-425-3

ELSS

CONTENTS

INTRODUCTION

[Jesus] summoned the Twelve and began to send them out two by two and gave them authority over unclean spirits. . . . So they went off and preached repentance. They drove out many demons, and they anointed with oil many who were sick and cured them. . . .

The apostles gathered together with Jesus and reported all they had done and taught. He said to them, "Come away by yourselves to a deserted place and rest a while."
—Mark 6:7, 12–13, 30–31

AGAIN AND AGAIN IN THE GOSPEL ACCOUNTS, WE read about how Jesus gathers his disciples. When they are chosen for a mission, Jesus gathers them together. When the mission is done, he gathers them again to rest. When they are weary after disappointment or joyful after success, when they are afraid, or when they are arguing with each other, he calls them together to teach them, to commission them, or just to be with them. In all their beginnings and all their endings, the disciples come together to be with Jesus.

That pattern continues today. We are Christ's disciples, and he continues to call us together to be with him and learn from him—because that is what happens every time we celebrate the liturgy. Christ is the one who gathers us; it is Christ who teaches us; Christ feeds us with his Body and Blood; and Christ is the one who sends us out on mission.

> ◆ **Taking part in the Eucharistic sacrifice, the source and summit of the Christian life, [the people of God] offer the divine victim to God and themselves along with him.**
>
> —*Dogmatic Constitution on the Church (Lumen gentium)*, 11

When we come together at liturgy, we are responding to the invitation of Jesus to "come away . . . and rest awhile."[1] The liturgy gathers us together in moments of joy and moments of intense sadness, as well as in the midst of our everyday lives. The liturgy, especially the Mass, is not only for special occasions. It is meant to be part of the rhythm of our lives—part of our ordinariness. At the same time, it is big enough to take in all we mourn and all we celebrate.

The bishops who met during the Second Vatican Council (1962–1965) described the liturgy in this way:

> The liturgy is the *summit* toward which the activity of the Church is directed; at the same time it is the *fount* [source] from which all the Church's power flows. For the aim and object of apostolic works is that all who are made children of God by faith and baptism should come together to praise God in the midst of his Church, to take part in the sacrifice, and to eat the Lord's Supper.

> The liturgy in its turn moves the faithful . . . the renewal in the eucharist of the covenant between the Lord and his people draws the faithful into the compelling love of Christ and sets them on fire. From the liturgy, therefore, particularly from the eucharist, grace is poured forth upon us as from a fountain.[2]

This is an extraordinary statement. The liturgy is the "fount," the source, for everything the Church does? Everything? All the preaching, ministering, serving, nursing, caring, feeding, teaching, advocating? And all of that activity in turn is directed towards the liturgy?

In this book, we're going to explore what it means to call the liturgy the "source and summit."[3] What is the liturgy? What happens when we celebrate the Eucharist together? How is Christ present in the liturgy? And what does the celebration of the liturgy call us to believe, to be, and to do?

❖ Questions for Discussion and Reflection

1. Sunday Mass is more than obligation; it is the high point of our Christian lives, the fullest expression of our identity as Christ's disciples. Does it feel this way to you? Why or why not?

2. Do you find Mass interesting? Boring? Soothing? Frustrating? What makes you react the way you do?

3. What do you need to learn about in order to appreciate the Mass more fully?

4. Is participating in Sunday Mass an important part of your relationship with God?

About the Author

Corinna Laughlin is the pastoral assistant for liturgy at St. James Cathedral in Seattle, Washington, and liturgy consultant for the Archdiocese of Seattle. She has written extensively on the liturgy for Liturgy Training Publications, an agency of the Archdiocese of Chicago, and has contributed articles to *Pastoral Liturgy*®, *Ministry and Liturgy*, and other publications. She holds a doctorate in English from the University of Washington.

About the Artist

Lalo Garcia has spent thirty-five years immersed in the world of art. Garcia's love for his native culture, combined with his faith and his commitment to preserving the folklore of Mexico, is reflected in his unique compositions. Garcia's work has been permanently placed in sacred spaces throughout the United States. Garcia is one of eleven commissioned artists selected by the Archdiocese of Los Angeles to create artwork for the Los Angeles Cathedral of the Angels. His website is www.LaloGarcia.com.

Chapter 1
What Is Liturgy?

TAKE A LOOK AT THE COVER OF THIS BOOK AND the painting by Lalo Garcia. The artist shows us a wonderful scene, rich in symbols. At the center is an altar, where we see a priest elevating the host and the chalice, while a deacon stands next to him, holding up the *Book of the Gospels*. We know just what is happening: the Mass! But the image does not stop there. From the altar pours a river, which flows through the landscape, down from the mountain and into the distance. People old and young climb the mountain and hurry down again. This, too, is an image of the Mass! The painting by Lalo Garcia is an illustration of one of the key teachings of the Second Vatican Council about the liturgy: the liturgy is the "summit toward which the activity of the Church is directed" and also the "fount [the source] from which all the Church's power flows."[1] The liturgy is a mountain.

Think of some of the mountaintop moments in the Bible. In the Book of Exodus, Moses encounters God at the mountain of Horeb. Later, God reveals himself to the Israelites on another mountain, Sinai. In the Gospel according to Matthew, Jesus takes his disciples up the Mount of Beatitudes to teach them. On Mount Tabor he is transfigured in the presence of Peter, James, and John; and on the hill of Calvary, he is crucified. In the Scriptures, mountains are places of closeness to God. On mountains, we can even touch God, in his most sublime divinity and in his most vulnerable humanity.

For Christians, the liturgy—and especially the Mass—is the mountain we climb, day by day, Sunday after Sunday, to encounter God as did the Israelites of old, to meet Christ and learn from him as the disciples did. In the liturgy, Christians glimpse the fulfillment of Isaiah's prophecy:

> The mountain of the LORD's house
> shall be established as the highest mountain
> and raised above the hills.
> All nations shall stream toward it.[2]

In the liturgy, we climb the mountain to gather in God's presence, to listen to God's Word, to be transformed.

What Does *Liturgy* Mean?

The word "liturgy" comes from a Greek word meaning "public work" or "work of the people." In the ancient world, the word was used to refer to a variety of forms of service on behalf of the community. In the New Testament, the same Greek word, *leitourgia* (or *leitourgos*), is used in a number of different contexts, and translated in various ways:

❖ Luke 1:23: "When his [Zechariah's] days of **ministry** were completed, he went home."

❖ Acts of the Apostles 13:2: "While they were worshiping the Lord and fasting, the holy Spirit said, 'Set apart for me Barnabas and Saul for the **work** to which I have called them.'"

❖ Romans 15:16: "A minister of Christ Jesus to the Gentiles in performing the **priestly service** of the gospel of God."

❖ 2 Corinthians 9:12: "The administration of this **public service** is not only supplying the needs of the holy ones but is also overflowing in many acts of thanksgiving to God."

❖ Philippians 2:17: "Even if I am poured out as a libation upon the sacrificial **service** of your faith, I rejoice and share my joy with all of you."[3]

◆ In the East, the word "liturgy" became specifically associated with the celebration of the Eucharist. Orthodox Christians speak not of "Mass" but of "Divine Liturgy." In the West, however, the word largely disappeared from use: Catholics used terms like "office," "rite," and most especially, "Mass," to describe their public worship. It was not until the study of the history of Christian worship really got underway in the nineteenth century that the word "liturgy" reentered the Catholic vocabulary.

In these different contexts, the word *liturgy* is used to refer to priestly ministry, service of the poor, and the proclamation of the Gospel. Elsewhere in the New Testament, *liturgy* is even used to describe Jesus himself, who is called the one *leitourgos*, "who has taken his seat at the right hand of the throne of the Majesty in heaven, a **minister** of the sanctuary and of the true tabernacle."[4] In the New Testament, *liturgy* is any form of sacred service, offered on behalf of the people.

What Liturgy Is . . .

Today, when we talk about "liturgy," we mean the public worship prescribed by the Church—the sacraments, especially the Eucharist, and the Liturgy of the Hours. When the Church celebrates the liturgy, Christ is present in a special way. In fact, whenever the Church celebrates the liturgy, Christ is not only present, Christ *presides*—it is his prayer: "Christ is always present in his Church, especially in its liturgical celebrations. . . . Rightly, then, the liturgy is considered as an exercise of the priestly office of Jesus Christ."[5] In the liturgy, we pray with and in Christ.

How is that possible? Because the Church is conformed to Christ. If we look at the deeds of Jesus as they are described in the New Testament, we recognize that Jesus was a **priest**—most especially when he offered the gift of himself on the altar of the Cross. He was also a **prophet**, proclaiming the coming of the Kingdom of God, speaking the truth through words and symbolic actions like the prophets Elijah, Jeremiah, and Isaiah had done before him. And Jesus was a **king**, anointed by the Holy Spirit. But Jesus is a new kind of king, a servant king, a suffering king, whose crown is made of thorns. We glimpse the different aspects of Christ's ministry in some of the names by which he is called in the Gospel accounts: the same Jesus is "Son of Man," "Son of David," and "Son of God."

> ◆ **As Christ was anointed Priest, Prophet, and King, so may you live always as members of his body, sharing everlasting life.**
> —*Rite of Baptism for Children*, 62

In the celebration of the Sacrament of Baptism, after the immersion in or pouring of water, every new Christian is anointed with sacred chrism. The priest or deacon prays that we might "live always as members" of the Body of Christ who is "Priest, Prophet, and King."[6] Like Jesus, who was the Messiah, the anointed one, we are also anointed. And we are anointed not to do something quite different from what Jesus did, but to do just what Jesus did—to share in his mission as priest, prophet, and king. When we who are the Church gather to pray, Christ prays.

At every liturgy, it is Christ, our high priest, who presides, and the Church—the priestly people of God—joins him in the offering. Because of Christ's presence and action in the liturgy, the Church teaches that "every liturgical celebration . . . is a sacred action surpassing all others; no other action of the Church can equal its effectiveness by the same title and to the same degree."[7]

> It is Christ, our high priest, who presides. ❖

. . . And What Liturgy Isn't

Some familiar Catholic prayers are not liturgy. Devotional practices, like the Rosary and the Divine Mercy Chaplet, novena prayers, the Way of the Cross, and *Tre Ore* services on Good Friday, are not liturgy. Even though they follow a prescribed pattern, and can sometimes be led in public by the priest or bishop—even by the pope!—that does not make them equal to the liturgy. These devotions can be an immensely valuable part of the prayer life of the faithful. Praying the Rosary can draw us closer to Mary, and meditating on the mysteries can help us to reflect on and understand the life of Jesus and Mary more deeply. Praying the Divine Mercy Chaplet can draw us into the mystery of Christ and intensify our observance of the Easter Octave, the eight days between Easter Sunday and the Second Sunday of Easter (Divine Mercy Sunday). But these devotions should enhance our participation in the liturgy and point us towards the liturgy, never act as a substitute for it. Nothing can replace the public worship of the Church, because no prayer is more important than the liturgy.

And there's more to say about what liturgy isn't. Liturgy isn't just the externals—the rubrics (detailed instructions) printed in the books that are used at the various liturgical rites, such as *The Roman Missal*, which includes the texts of the priest's prayers for the Mass, or the *Lectionary for Mass*, which includes the readings. Nor is liturgy simply the music, the processions, and the ritual actions. All of these are important, but liturgy is more. Liturgy includes a lived dimension. In order to fully experience what the liturgy is, we have to enter into it, participate in it, and experience it. Liturgy includes many important words and prayers, but liturgy is not what can be written down on paper. Liturgy happens when rituals and prayers are led by a minister in the midst of the people of God. Liturgy, in other words, is more verb than noun!

What Are the Liturgies of the Church?

Our sacramental encounters with Christ, first and foremost in the Mass, are the principal liturgies of the Church. These include celebrations of all the sacraments: Baptism, Confirmation, Eucharist, Penance, Anointing of the Sick, Holy Orders, and Matrimony. Every time one of the sacraments is celebrated—whether it is a solemn Mass in a cathedral, confessions at a stadium at World Youth Day, or the Anointing of the Sick given in a noisy hospital— the liturgy of the Church is happening.

> The liturgy extends beyond the celebration of the sacraments. ❖

The liturgy extends beyond the celebration of the sacraments to the Liturgy of the Hours. Also called the Divine Office and sometimes the Breviary, in reference to the book that includes the offices, the Liturgy of the Hours is a sequence of prayers built around the rhythm of the day, with offices that are tied to specific times of the day, from Morning Prayer to Night Prayer. The Liturgy of the Hours is part of an ancient tradition and is obligatory for bishops, priests, and religious. Through the Liturgy of the Hours, the Church observes Christ's injunction to pray without ceasing[8] and sanctifies each day, and each hour, with prayer and praise of God.

People are often surprised to learn that the great advocate for the poor, Dorothy Day, with Peter Maurin the founder of the Catholic Worker Movement, was also keenly interested in the liturgy. In the late 1930s, she introduced the praying of Compline (Night Prayer) at the Catholic Worker houses in New York City. At that time, most laypeople had never experienced the Liturgy of the Hours before. Some felt that this prayer should be left to the monks in the monasteries, but Day felt it was important not only to pray, but to pray in union with the whole Church throughout the world. That is the power of liturgy!

The celebrations of each of the sacraments, the Liturgy of the Hours—all of these are liturgies of the Church. But the celebration of the Eucharist is the most important. In the celebration of the Mass, we encounter Christ, and we see most clearly what the Church is, or rather, *who* the Church is. In the liturgy, we discover that we *are* the Church when we come together as a community in prayer and worship. The Mass is the Church's prayer, and it is our prayer: in the words of the Second Vatican Council, the Eucharist "is the outstanding means whereby the faithful may express in their lives and manifest to others the mystery of Christ and the real nature of the true Church."[9] Something happens when we celebrate the Mass, to us as a community and to each of us as individuals.

> ◆ **The excellence of Christian prayer lies in its sharing in the reverent love of the only-begotten Son for the Father and in the prayer that the Son put into words in his earthly life and that still continues without ceasing in the name of the whole human race and for its salvation, throughout the universal Church and in all its members.**
>
> —General Instruction of the Liturgy of the Hours, 7

Do Other Christian Denominations Celebrate the Liturgy?

In describing Christian worship, the terms "liturgical" and "nonliturgical" are frequently used. Nonliturgical denominations are those whose worship services do not follow a prescribed pattern. An example would be the Religious Society of Friends (the Quakers), famous for their "waiting worship." People gather for a meeting and there is no plan for what will happen, no beginning, middle, or end. The attendees simply sit in prayer and speak when God's spirit moves them to do so. To describe these traditions as nonliturgical is not to suggest that they are unorganized or purely spontaneous—even Quaker waiting worship is not entirely unpredictable in how it unfolds—but it is a helpful way of distinguishing their forms of worship from those of the liturgical traditions, like Catholic and Orthodox Churches as well as Lutheran, Episcopal, or Anglican churches, among others, which follow carefully prescribed and often quite ancient forms.

How Did Christian Liturgy Develop?

Jesus was part of a rich liturgical tradition. In fact, the Gospel accounts frequently describe Jesus and his disciples participating in Jewish public worship. On the Sabbath, Jesus goes to the synagogue.[10] He and his disciples go up to Jerusalem for solemn feast days.[11] They celebrate the Passover.[12] The disciples even delay their visit to the tomb of their dead Teacher in observance of the Sabbath rest.[13]

The earliest Christians were Jewish believers who continued to worship in the synagogue and visit the Temple in Jerusalem: "Every day they devoted themselves to meeting together in the temple area and to breaking bread in their homes."[14] Practices ancient and new were observed side by side without any sense of contradiction between the two. For them, following Jesus flowed directly from their Jewish identity and practice. But conflict was quick to come. As the Gospel spread to non-Jewish peoples, the question arose of how much of the Jewish law these Gentiles would need to observe—if any. This controversy figures largely in the Acts of the Apostles and in some of the New Testament letters. Meanwhile, Jewish followers of Jesus began to be persecuted by their own religious leaders. These two sources of tension in early Christianity led to rapid change. Christians developed a liturgy of their own, built on the foundation of Jewish worship, with readings from the Old Testament and the singing of the psalms. The early Christians prayed in Greek, the most widely understood language of the time, but Hebrew, the language of the Bible, and Aramaic, the language of Jesus and his disciples, continued to be used in their prayer: *Alleluia! Marana tha! Ephphetha!*

Christian worship soon began to take on its own distinctive shape: "They devoted themselves to the teaching of the apostles and to the communal life, to the breaking of the bread and to the prayers."[15] Within a very few years after the Resurrection of Jesus, the basic pattern of the liturgy today—readings, prayers, Eucharist—is evident. By the middle of the second century, the Christian community was clearly a liturgical one. In his *First Apology*, written about AD 155, St. Justin Martyr describes the Christian worship he experienced:

> On Sunday we have a common assembly of all our members, whether they live in the city or in the outlying districts. The recollections of the apostles or the writings of the prophets are read, as long as there is time. When the reader has finished, the president of the assembly speaks to us; he urges everyone to imitate the examples of virtue we have heard in the readings. Then we all stand up together and pray.
>
> On the conclusion of our prayer, bread and wine and water are brought forward. The president offers prayers and gives thanks to the best of his ability, and the people give their assent by saying, "Amen." The eucharist is distributed, everyone communicates, and the deacons take it to those who are absent.[16]

The liturgy St. Justin described is still clearly recognizable:

* gathering on Sunday
* readings from Scripture—the "prophets" and "Apostles"
* homily—"the president speaks to us"
* Prayer of the Faithful—"we all stand up together and pray"
* bread and wine are brought forward
* Eucharistic Prayer—"the president offers prayers"
* all say "Amen"
* the Eucharist is distributed

Through the centuries, this basic shape remained the same. But over time, the focus shifted away from the assembly of the faithful gathered for the prayer. When Latin replaced Greek as the language of the liturgy, it was because it was the most widely-spoken vernacular language in the ancient world. But as time passed, the Church continued to use Latin even though it had become obsolete in life outside the Church. People stopped participating because they could no longer understand what was said. Eventually, many of the lay faithful were entirely silent at Mass. Over the centuries, liturgy became more and more removed from the sense of a communal offering. The sense of the people's participation in the offering never disappeared entirely, but it became less direct, less clear.

At many Masses, prayers that had once been spoken aloud began to be spoken quietly by the priest. The responses which had once belonged to the entire community—"and with your spirit" and "we lift them up to the Lord," for example—were often said in low voices by the acolytes alone. A shift away from the people was reflected in church architecture, too, as open spaces gave way to more enclosed ones. In large cathedrals and monastic churches, the sanctuary would be separated from the nave by walls of wood or stone, with rood screens which were often splendid works of art but which partially or entirely blocked the view of the altar from the laity.

Well-educated people continued to pray with the Church. Museums and archives around the world house wonderful medieval books of hours, which would have been used by wealthy laypeople to pray the Liturgy of the Hours. But most people had no access to books, or to the education required to read in Latin. They turned to devotions like the Rosary, which developed as an alternative to the Liturgy of the Hours (praying all fifteen decades of the Rosary would add up to 150 Hail Marys, paralleling the 150 psalms in the Book of Psalms).

Renewal of the Liturgy

In the nineteenth century, scholars began to dig into the history of Catholic worship—and to discover a quite different vision. They began to use the term "liturgy" in speaking of the prayer of the Church. The word itself brought a subtle shift in emphasis—terms like "rites" and "offices" put the emphasis on rubrics, texts, and ministers, but "liturgy" puts the focus on the "work of the people" in making their offering to God. Gradually, the participation of the faithful became the focus and the rallying cry of the Liturgical Movement.

We call it the Liturgical Movement today, but it was not an organized movement. Rather, it was a loose group of scholars, pastors, and laypeople in many different settings—and many countries—who shared

> The liturgy . . . is the place where we come closest to Christ. ❖

a common belief that the renewal of the liturgy could change the lives of the Catholic faithful for the better. Pope Pius XI, Pope Pius XII, and Pope John XXIII all supported the work of the Liturgical Movement.

When the Second Vatican Council convened in October 1962, liturgy was the first topic discussed. The bishops at the Council discussed and debated many aspects of the liturgy, and gradually the first document of the Council, the *Constitution on the Sacred Liturgy*, was approved and issued. This document laid out a clear and inspiring vision for the Church's liturgy. Like the United States Constitution, the *Constitution on the Sacred Liturgy* does not include a lot of detail. Instead, it lays out the basic principles for the liturgy. The *Constitution* is the most quoted document in this book, and it is indispensable for anyone who wants to understand the Church's priorities when it comes to the liturgy. The *Constitution* emphasizes how important the liturgy is, because it is the place where we come closest to Christ, and puts great emphasis on the participation of the faithful in the Mass. The *Constitution* laid the groundwork for the liturgical reforms which ultimately gave us the liturgy as we celebrate it today.

The key principles in the *Constitution* are clear: The liturgy is of supreme importance in the life of the Church. The liturgy is the redemption made present, here and now. The liturgy is the primary way we express our identity as Catholics.[17] As such, the liturgy is not something we passively witness: it demands our active engagement.

What, Then, Is Liturgy?

Liturgy is cosmic. The liturgy takes the most fundamental elements of human life—our bodies, voices, minds, hearts—and the things that sustain us—water, light, oil, food, drink—and imbues them with enormous meaning. Liturgy draws in the ordinary—bread and wine; people like us!—so that God can transform them into his very presence. Through the liturgy, we come to recognize that the entire universe is signed with the presence of Christ. The seeds are everywhere; in the liturgy we see them burst into fruition. Whether we realize it or not, "in him we live and move and have our being."[18]

Liturgy is the official worship of the Church. It is not free-form. It is governed by universal norms. And yet, it is almost infinitely variable, and the familiar shape of the liturgy can take many tones and accommodate many languages, many styles of music, and many cultural approaches. The liturgy is not a private devotion: while I am deeply involved, it is not "my" prayer, nor is it "Father's" or "Bishop's." It is the Church's prayer. Liturgy, to be fully celebrated, requires both priest and people. Our presence is not optional, and while we surely benefit spiritually from Mass whether we are present or not, when absent we would not fulfill our responsibility to join the community of the Church in prayer. Liturgy, as a communal act, not only gathers a community, but helps to form a community. The act of being together at table, as we are when we gather for

> ◆ Joined to the incarnate Son, present in the Eucharist, the whole cosmos gives thanks to God. Indeed the Eucharist is itself an act of cosmic love: "Yes, cosmic! Because even when it is celebrated on the humble altar of a country church, the Eucharist is always in some way celebrated on the altar of the world." Eucharist joins heaven and earth; it embraces and penetrates all creation.
>
> —On Care for Our Common Home (Laudato si'), 236

> Liturgy . . . helps to form community. ❖

the Eucharist, of sharing the Word of God together, of being one in our sung and spoken prayers—all of these help us to recognize ourselves as a family of believers, the Body of Christ, and thus to be united in our action outside of the church as well.

❖ Questions for Discussion and Reflection

1. How is praying with a community different from praying on your own? Why do you think Jesus calls us to pray in both ways?

2. What do you hope to get out of this study of the liturgy?

3. What liturgies of the Church do you participate in on a regular basis?

4. Do you find that participating in the liturgy has an impact on your life outside of the liturgy?

5. If you had to explain to a non-Christian what the liturgy is for, what would you say?

6. Are there times when liturgy grabs and engages you? Are there times when you get bored?

7. What changes to the way the liturgy is celebrated have you experienced in your lifetime? How did those changes impact you? How did you respond?

Chapter 2
Liturgy Is an Encounter with Christ

T WO TRAVELERS ARE ON THEIR WAY TO THE
mountain. They seem to have paused for a moment, stopped in
their tracks by what they see. They reach out in a gesture that suggests
openness and amazement, recognition and gratitude.

The two travelers in the art of Lalo Garcia recall another pair of
travelers in the Gospel according to Luke. On the evening of the first
Easter Sunday, two disciples of Jesus are on their way out of Jerusalem.

It has been a devastating week in which they have witnessed their beloved teacher and friend arrested, subjected to trial in the religious and civil courts, and sentenced to death. As they walk away, trying to process all that has happened, a stranger comes up and walks and talks with them. Only after the stranger breaks bread with them do they recognize that this is Jesus himself, risen from the dead. "And it happened that, while he was with them at table, he took bread, said the blessing, broke it, and gave it to them. With that their eyes were opened and they recognized him, but he vanished from their sight. Then they said to each other, 'Were not our hearts burning [within us] while he spoke to us on the way and opened the scriptures to us?'"[1] Like the two pilgrims in the painting, the disciples on the road to Emmaus recognize the presence of Christ. And their response is wonder, openness, joy, and praise.

The story of Emmaus has deep resonance with the movement of the Eucharistic liturgy: Jesus is present with his disciples; he explains the Scriptures to them; he makes himself known in a special way in the breaking of bread; what they have heard and experienced sends them on a mission. The Eucharist follows the same pattern. We gather; Christ is with us. We listen to the Christ's Word. We share a meal made sacred by Christ's presence. We are sent forth.

> ◆ **At Sunday Mass, Christians relive with particular intensity the experience of the apostles on the evening of Easter when the Risen Lord appeared to them as they were gathered together.**
> —*On Keeping the Lord's Day Holy* (*Dies Domini*), 33

But there is another layer to discover in the Emmaus story. This encounter takes place shortly after the Crucifixion of Jesus, and the Crucifixion is what they talk about along the way. The mysterious stranger explains why it was "necessary" that the Messiah should suffer what Jesus suffered in Jerusalem in order to enter "glory." As he explains the Scriptures, he does so in light of the dying and rising of the Messiah—"he interpreted to them what referred to him in all the scriptures." The Christ who is revealed to them in the breaking of the bread is different from the Christ they knew before: this is the Risen Christ. The dying and rising of the Messiah has changed everything: the way the Scriptures are read and understood and the way Christ is recognized by his followers. This transformational event—the passion, death, and Resurrection of Christ—is called the Paschal Mystery. The liturgy of the Church is all about the Paschal Mystery.

What Do We Mean When We Say "Mystery"?

In general parlance, a "mystery" is something we haven't figured out yet, but usually can. At the end of a mystery novel, there is no mystery left to be solved! But in the Church, "mystery" means something quite different. It's not only something we haven't solved, but by its very nature, it's something that cannot be solved or fully understood. In the ancient world, the word "mystery" was used to describe rites or cults that were kept secret from all except the initiated (as in the Eleusinian Mysteries of ancient Greece). Christians adopted the word "mystery" as they sought to understand all that had happened to Jesus. St. Paul proclaims "God's wisdom, mysterious, hidden,"[2] and exclaims, "undeniably great is the mystery of devotion."[3] The central mystery of Christianity is Christ himself, "manifested in the flesh, / vindicated in the spirit, / seen by angels."[4]

> The central mystery of Christianity is Christ. ❖

What Is the Paschal Mystery?

The word "paschal" comes from the Greek word *pascha*, which derives from *pesach*, the Hebrew word for Passover. It refers to the "Passover" of Christ—his passion, death, and Resurrection, the work God sent him to accomplish. The Paschal Mystery is everything: it is the reason for our faith, the source of our life. "If Christ has not been raised, your faith is vain," St. Paul wrote to the Corinthians, and "we are the most pitiable people of all."[5] This central reality of our faith is a historical fact, but it is more than that too. Other historical events, even tremendously important ones, happen once and then begin to recede in the rearview mirror of time. But the Paschal Mystery is different. It *continues* to happen. The dying and rising of Christ is a living, ever-present reality which is still unfolding. That is why, during the great Vigil on the night before Easter, the Church repeats over and over again, "This is the night!"[6] Pope Benedict XVI said it this way: "The Resurrection is not a thing of the past, the Resurrection has reached us and seized us. We grasp hold of it, we grasp hold of the risen Lord, and we know that he holds us firmly even when our hands grow weak."[7] To be a Christian is to be caught up into the Paschal Mystery, to be inseparably and intimately connected with the dying and rising of Christ.

How Does the Liturgy Celebrate the Paschal Mystery?

Of course, the Paschal Mystery of Christ is celebrated in a particular way at Easter. In many languages, this connection is clear from the very name of the Easter feast: *Pascha* (Latin); *Pascha* (Greek); *Pâques* (French); *Pasqua* (Italian); *Pascua* (Spanish); *Paskah* (Indonesian); *Paskha* (Russian); *Påsk* (Swedish).

> Liturgy . . . is about the Paschal mystery. ❖

But Easter is not the only time the liturgy celebrates the Paschal Mystery. In fact, every Mass in every season is about the Paschal Mystery, because every time we celebrate the Eucharist we recall Christ's death and Resurrection, and receive his Risen Body. On saints' days and on days honoring the Blessed Virgin Mary, what we are ultimately celebrating is the Paschal Mystery—Christ's victory over death is reflected in their lives and is the source of their holiness. At funerals, we celebrate the Paschal Mystery as we pray that the deceased, who was joined to Christ by Baptism, now share fully in his risen life.

The same word, *mystery*, is used in reference both to the Paschal Mystery and to the celebration of that reality in the liturgy. The Prayer over the Offerings on Holy Thursday is an ancient prayer that expresses the inextricable link between the Paschal Mystery and the liturgy:

Grant us, O Lord, we pray,
that we may participate worthily
in these mysteries,
for whenever the memorial of this sacrifice
is celebrated,
the work of our redemption is accomplished.

The liturgy is "the memorial," the solemn remembering of the sacrifice of Christ, and when we celebrate the liturgy, "the work of our redemption is accomplished"—Christ's saving work is underway, now. Why is the liturgy so important? Because here, the Paschal Mystery is both remembered and made present—close enough to touch.

Where Do We Encounter Christ in the Liturgy?

Christ is always present at the liturgy, acting with us and in us. The *Constitution on the Sacred Liturgy* highlights four "presences" of Christ—four ways in which we encounter Christ in the liturgy. We meet Christ in all four of these presences at Mass, the most important liturgy the Church celebrates. But Christ is present in all the liturgies of the Church, not just at Mass. When we pray the Liturgy of the Hours or participate in Benediction of the Blessed Sacrament, receive the Anointing of the Sick in a hospital or go to confession, commit the body of a loved one to the earth in the Rite of Committal or receive one of the many blessings of the Church—we are celebrating the Church's liturgy, and thus we are encountering one or more of the "presences" of Christ.

Christ is always present at the liturgy. ❖

Christ Is Present in the Eucharist

In the Eucharist, we encounter the Real Presence of Christ. It is not called "Real Presence" because the other presences of Christ are somehow less real, but to emphasize the special way in which Christ is present in this sacrament. We believe that the bread and wine we place on the altar become the Body and Blood of Christ through the action of the Holy Spirit. We call this change "transubstantiation," but knowing the name for it does not mean we understand it. Indeed, the liturgy speaks of the Eucharist in terms that express awe in the presence of a profound mystery: the prayers of the Mass include words like "wonderful," "mystery," "sweetness," and "delight" in speaking of the Eucharist.[8] As Pope St. John Paul II has written, "we are constantly tempted to reduce the Eucharist to our own dimensions, while in reality *it is we who must open ourselves up to the dimensions of the Mystery*."[9]

> ◆ **In the most blessed sacrament of the Eucharist "the body and blood, together with the soul and divinity, of our Lord Jesus Christ and, therefore, *the whole Christ is truly, really, and substantially contained*."**
>
> —*Catechism of the Catholic Church*, 1374[*]

St. Thomas Aquinas wrote about the mystery of Christ's presence in the Eucharist in theological treatises as well as in prayers and poems. His hymn in honor of the Blessed Sacrament is often heard as the sequence on the Solemnity of the Most Holy Body and Blood of Christ (Corpus Christi): "Sight has fail'd, nor thought conceives, / But a dauntless faith believes, / Resting on a pow'r divine."[10]

In a unique way that the Church has meditated on for centuries, Christ is substantially present in the Eucharistic elements of bread and wine: he is "true food," and "true drink."[11] This abiding presence changes everything, even how we move around the altar and the tabernacle. It is reflected in how we approach the sacrament when we come forward for Communion. It should be reflected in how we treat those with whom we become one through the sacrament as well.

Christ Is Present in the Word

Christ "is present in his word, since it is he himself who speaks when the holy Scriptures are read in the Church."[12] In the liturgy described by St. Justin in the first chapter of this book,[13] the reading of the Old and New Testaments was a prominent part of the Sunday gathering

---

[*] Quoting the Council of Trent (1551): Denzinger-Schonmetzer, *Enchiridion Symbolorum, definitionum et declarationum de rebus fidei et morum*, 1651.

for the early Christians. Scripture never stopped being an important part of the liturgy—there were never less than two readings, typically an Epistle (a reading from one of the New Testament letters) and a Gospel—but as fewer and fewer people understood Latin, the faithful had limited access to this form of Christ's presence.

The Second Vatican Council brought the Scriptures back to the heart of the liturgy. "The treasures of the Bible are to be opened up more lavishly," the bishops of the Council wrote, "so that a richer share in God's word may be provided for the faithful."[14] The Church has certainly answered that call. The revised *Lectionary for Mass*, which appeared following the Council, increased the number of readings to be proclaimed at liturgy. At Sunday Mass, in addition to the Epistle reading and the Gospel, an Old Testament reading and a Responsorial Psalm were added. Furthermore, the one-year cycle of readings was expanded to a three-year cycle of readings, allowing for almost all of the New Testament and a good portion of the Old Testament to be proclaimed at Sunday Mass. A two-year Lectionary was prepared for weekday Masses, expanding the amount of Scripture proclaimed in the liturgy even more.

The function of the Lectionary is not chiefly educational: we listen to the Scriptures not to learn about the past, but to encounter Christ in the present. In the Gospel according to Luke, Jesus goes into the synagogue in his

> ◆ [Christ] is present in his word, since it is he himself who speaks when the holy Scriptures are read in the Church.
>
> —*Constitution on the Sacred Liturgy (Sacrosanctum concilium)*, 7

hometown and proclaims a passage from the prophet Isaiah. Then he tells those gathered, "today this scripture passage is fulfilled in your hearing."[15] This is the attitude of the Church as we listen to the proclamation of the Scriptures at Mass: we read as Jesus himself did, seeking the "today," the fulfillment of the Scriptures in our own lives.

Christ speaks to us when both the Old and New Testament readings are proclaimed. Like Jesus in the synagogue at Nazareth, or on the road to Emmaus with his downcast disciples, we continue to ponder the Old Testament. We never outgrow it: but we read the Old Testament in the light of the Risen Christ, who, "beginning with Moses and all the prophets, . . . interpreted to them what referred to him in all the scriptures."[16] In the pages of the Old Testament, we discover who Jesus is, for "the New Testament lies hidden in the Old; the Old Testament comes fully to light in the New."[17]

The Gospel is where the presence of Christ is most palpable. While we honor all the Scriptures as the revealed Word of God, the Church hears the Gospel accounts as the voice of Christ himself. In the liturgy, we highlight the reading of the Gospel in special ways. We stand to listen. We sing "Alleluia," an acclamation of praise. Candles are carried and sometimes the book from which the Gospel is proclaimed is carried in procession and honored with sweet-smelling incense. The reading is proclaimed by an ordained minister, the deacon or priest, who kisses the words of the Gospel after reading them. All of these help to draw our attention to Christ's presence in the Gospel, the high point of the Liturgy of the Word.

Christ Is Present in His Minister

Whenever the Church gathers to pray, it is Christ who presides. Christ is present in the priest or bishop who, by his ordination, shares in the priestly office of Christ. During the liturgy, the celebrant is said to act *in persona Christi capitis,* a Latin phrase which means "in the person of Christ, the head." Through the celebrant's words and gestures, Christ makes the sacraments living and effective for the faithful who receive them: "when a man baptizes," the Second Vatican Council reminds us, "it is really Christ himself who baptizes."[18]

> ◆ To form a priestly people you appoint ministers of Christ your Son by the power of the Holy Spirit, arranging them in different orders.
>
> —*Rite of Ordination of Priests,* 131

How can a man act in the person of Christ? The priest can do this not because of his holiness, but in spite of his weakness. The presence of Christ in the minister is not a shield that protects him from the weakness and error that afflict the rest of us. He can still sin, and that sin can get in the way of his ministry to God's people. But the power of the Holy Spirit is greater than human weakness and sin, and ensures that Christ is present and active in the Church's sacraments, even when they are conferred by a sinful minister.

We acknowledge Christ's presence in the minister in various ways in the liturgy. He sits in a special chair, a sign of the teaching office he receives from Christ. The chasuble, the special vestment worn only for the celebration of the Mass, sets him apart and highlights the unique ministry he fulfills when he celebrates Mass, acting in the person of Christ.

Christ Is Present in the Assembly

Christ is present "when the Church prays and sings, for he promised: 'Where two or three are gathered together in my name, there am I in the midst of them.'"[19] There is something special about a liturgical assembly. By our Baptism, each of us has become a temple of the Holy Spirit; each of us has been given a share in Christ's mission as priest, prophet, and king. But this new creation does not touch us only as individuals. It draws us into a community of believers. It makes us members of the one Body of Christ. We are more than the sum of our parts, because when the baptized come together, Christ himself is present.

Gathering together is a consistent pattern in the ministry of Jesus. When a huge crowd followed him, Jesus responded to their needs, teaching them and healing their sick. The disciples urged him to scatter the people: "dismiss the crowds so that they can go to the villages and buy food for themselves."[20] But Jesus' response was different: "There is no need for them to go away; give them some food yourselves."[21] The prophet Isaiah spoke of a mountaintop where God would gather people of all nations for a feast of rich foods and choice wines.[22] In the gathering, healing, and feeding of the multitude by Jesus, this vision is fulfilled. In an unruly, hungry crowd, Jesus reveals a glimpse of God's reign.

For the early Christians, the gathering of the faithful was recognized as a sign of Christ's presence. An ancient text called *The Teaching of the Twelve Apostles* (or *Didache*) quotes what is perhaps an early Eucharistic Prayer: "As this broken bread scattered on the mountains was gathered and became one, so too, may your Church be gathered together from the ends of the earth into your kingdom."[23] The bread of the Eucharist, formed of many grains of wheat, is itself an image of the coming together of people from every nation into the Church. The community itself, like the bread broken and shared, is a sign of the transforming presence of Christ.

> The gathering of the faithful was recognized as a sign of Christ's presence. ❖

No wonder, then, that in the Book of Revelation, heaven is seen as a liturgical assembly at prayer: "I had a vision of a great multitude, which no one could count, from every nation, race, people, and tongue."[24] The gathering of believers is a true reflection of God's Kingdom, because Christ is present "when the Church prays and sings."[25]

How Do We Experience Christ's Presence in the Liturgy?

Christ is present in the liturgy: in the sacraments, in his Word, in the priest, in the gathering of the people. Christ is present in all these ways not simply to be looked at: Christ expects a response from us! How do we respond? "By both song and prayer."[26] Through our participation in the liturgy, we enter into dialogue with God. No wonder, then, that the participation of the faithful was the primary goal of the liturgical renewal called for by the Second Vatican Council:

> The Church earnestly desires that all the faithful be led to that *full, conscious,* and *active* participation in liturgical cele-brations called for by the very nature of the liturgy. Such participation by the Christian people as "a chosen race, a royal

priesthood, a holy nation, God's own people" (1 Peter 2:9; see 2:4–5) is their right and duty by reason of their baptism.[27]

What is meant by those three familiar words—full, conscious, and active?

Full participation does not mean that all of us are doing everything all the time. That would simply be more participation, not full participation! Full participation in the liturgy reaches within us and beyond us. To participate fully is to allow the liturgy to shape our lives until it reflects Christ's self-giving love—that pattern of taking, blessing, breaking, and giving—which is repeated again and again when we celebrate the Mass. *Full* participation in the liturgy is not something that can be measured. It does not just mean knowing the responses and singing the songs. Full participation happens when the liturgy feeds us and nourishes us and challenges us to be people for others.

Our participation in the liturgy must be *conscious*. To be conscious is to be aware, attentive. Conscious participation does not simply go through the motions, but is aware of the unfolding movement of the liturgy, seeking its meanings. Conscious participation is ready to encounter Christ in the liturgy. That means taking time to prepare for Mass as we would for other important events in our lives. We can prepare this through reading and study—reflecting on the Scriptures and on the texts and prayers of the liturgy itself. We can prepare through daily prayer, examining our own lives in light of the Gospel. These practices will help us get to know Christ as a friend and will train us to recognize Christ's presence in our lives. And preparation like this, in cooperation with the Holy Spirit, will lead us toward conscious participation in the Eucharist. The better we know Christ in our day-to-day lives, the more readily we will recognize and rejoice in his presence in the liturgy.

> To be conscious is to be aware, attentive. ❖

Finally, the liturgy calls for *active* participation. Liturgy isn't something that happens *to* us. Liturgy is not for spectators. Liturgy demands our engagement. Think of all the ways the liturgy engages us. We walk, we bow, we kneel, we genuflect, we sit, we stand. We raise our hands, we make the Sign of the Cross, we shake hands. We speak, we sing, we listen, we keep silence. We eat; we drink. Through these forms of active participation, we pray with our voices and with our bodies. Active participation in the liturgy is prayer incarnate—prayer that is embodied in us, with all our faults and limitations. Of course, active participation is not enough—all of us have had days where we simply went through the motions without being interiorly engaged with the liturgy. But active participation is essential. "Our participation in the Liturgy is challenging. Sometimes, our voices do not correspond to the convictions of our hearts. At other times, we are distracted or preoccupied by the cares of the world."[28] But the invitation to enter more deeply is always there. Whether we are ready for him or not, Christ is there for us, always calling us to enter more deeply into this shared prayer. When it comes to full, conscious, and active participation in the liturgy, we are always on the journey, both as individuals and as communities, because in the liturgy, the Holy Spirit is always revealing new layers of meaning to us.

> The liturgy is the action of Christ in and with the Church. ❖

The liturgy is not about receiving a holy *thing* but encountering a *person*, Jesus Christ. The liturgy is the action of Christ in and with the Church. Christ is present here: in the sacrament of his Body and Blood, in his word, in the priest, and in the gathered assembly. Christ speaks to us, comes to us, dwells with us. And we are called to respond to this encounter with all our being: voice, body, mind, heart—and action.

❖ Questions for Discussion and Reflection

1. Read the story of the journey to Emmaus in your Bible (Luke 24:13–35). The disciples realize that Christ was with them all along only in hindsight. Are there times or moments in your life where you realized only later that Christ was guiding you or revealing something to you?

2. Where and when do you feel closest to Christ?

3. Think about the four ways Christ is present in the liturgy—in the sacrament, in the word, in the priest, in the gathered assembly. Think of a time when you felt Christ's presence in each of these places.

4. Do you participate *fully* in the Mass? Are there areas of your life that seem cut off from your faith?

5. Do you participate *consciously* in the Mass? Are there parts of the Mass or the liturgy in general that confuse or puzzle you, that you would like to explore more fully?

6. Do you participate *actively* in the Mass? If not, why not? What holds you back?

Chapter 3

Liturgy Is a Marvelous Exchange between God and Humanity

LUMINOUS WATER FLOWS DOWN FROM THE ALTAR on the mountaintop, and rivulets branch out to water the land to the left and to the right. Three women stand at the river bank. While the child bathes or plays in the water, the older women gather it into a vessel. Generation after generation, this water renews and refreshes; it is a source of life and a source of delight. Look at the cover of this book:

you can see how the river flows through the landscape. Even the deer drink from it. This water gives life to all of creation.

In this painting, Lalo Garcia draws on ancient imagery. The Old Testament prophet Ezekiel describes a river flowing out from the right side of the Temple of God. Wherever the river flows, life springs forth: trees grow, fish abound, and even the polluted waters of the sea are purified when the river touches it.[1] In the New Testament, the Holy City is described in similar terms: "the angel showed me the river of life-giving water, sparkling like crystal, flowing from the throne of God and of the Lamb down the middle of its street."[2] Wherever the water flows, there is life, healing, and abundance. The river symbolizes the life-giving presence of God.

In the Gospel according to John, the evangelist describes in great detail what happens after Jesus' death:

> When they came to Jesus and saw that he was already dead, they did not break his legs, but one soldier thrust his lance into his side, and immediately blood and water flowed out. An eyewitness has testified, and his testimony is true; he knows that he is speaking the truth, so that you also may [come to] believe.[3]

Why does he dwell on this detail with such emphasis? John wants us to remember the rivers flowing forth from God's presence, touching and renewing the world. The blood and water flowing from the pierced side of Christ are the fulfillment of Ezekiel's vision, the source from which the Church draws its life.

> For raised up high on the Cross,
> he gave himself up for us with a wonderful love
> and poured out Blood and water from his pierced side,
> the wellspring of the Church's Sacraments,
> so that, won over to the open Heart of the Savior,
> all might draw water from the springs of salvation.[4]

In Christ, we touch the divine presence; in the liturgy, we approach the life-giving stream. We are washed with it in Baptism; we drink it in the Eucharist. The water that flows forth from God's presence is not there simply to be looked it: it is poured forth *for* us, to wash us, quench our thirst, and renew us. "With joy you will draw water / from the fountains of salvation" cries Isaiah.[5] In the liturgy, we do just that.

Liturgy and the Incarnation

We can touch Christ in the sacraments because Christ is God's eternal Word made flesh. The phrase "Incarnate Word" is so familiar to us that it can be hard to step back and realize how stunning it is. Words are words and things are things, right? Earth and heaven, human and divine: these are opposites— aren't they? Not anymore. Now that Christ has taken on our humanity, now that God has become human like us, everything is different. It is a new creation, and we are part of it.

Because of the Incarnation, we Catholics do not see material things as intrinsically evil; nor do we see our bodies as evil. The created world and all its creatures never cease to have the potential to be holy, because Christ's coming in human flesh sanctified humanity. By coming into the world and making use of things, Christ sanctified the world of things.

> ◆ The Lord, in the culmination of the mystery of the Incarnation, chose to reach our intimate depths through a fragment of matter. He comes not from above, but from within, he comes that we might find him in this world of ours. In the Eucharist, fullness is already achieved; it is the living center of the universe, the overflowing core of love and of inexhaustible life.
>
> —*On Care for Our Common Home (Laudato si')*, 236

The mystery of the Incarnation —of God coming in human flesh— has shaped the imagination of the Church. The Incarnation is why we worship the way we do. It's why we build dedicated church buildings. It's why beauty—music, art, architecture, vesture—has such an important place in our public worship. When Jesus became flesh and dwelt among us, he made it possible for this world to be holy. This is what the poet Gerard Manley Hopkins meant when he wrote, "The world is charged with the grandeur of God."[6]

In the Incarnation, Jesus broke down the wall between the divine and the human. No longer opposites, the human and the divine are now in constant relationship. An ancient prayer calls this new reality a "marvelous exchange": "O marvelous exchange! Man's Creator has become man, born of a virgin. We have been made sharers in the divinity of Christ who humbled himself to share in our humanity."[7] Christ takes on our humanity, and in exchange gives us a share in his divinity. This is truly a "marvelous exchange," in which Jesus gives us the best of the bargain.

> Liturgy expresses what we believe about the Incarnation. ❖

This exchange is not always easy. We often find the flesh to be in tension with the spirit. As Jesus said, "the spirit is willing, but the flesh is weak."[8] But we do not have a choice. We are embodied beings, and thus our prayer is also embodied: in this life, it is only in our bodies that we discover God. The Church exists in this same tension. "It is of the essence of the Church to be both human and divine," wrote the bishops of the Second Vatican Council, "present in this world yet not at home in it."[9]

This fruitful place of tension is where we live our lives of faith, and it is precisely where the liturgy happens, too. The liturgy is the embodied prayer that we offer on earth in union with heaven. The liturgy expresses what we believe about the Incarnation so well: in the liturgy, we experience the "marvelous exchange" on a daily basis. The liturgy is a constant ebb and flow, a joining together of earth and heaven. In the sacraments, the earthly becomes the vehicle for the divine: water for Baptism, oil for Confirmation and the Anointing of the Sick, bread and wine for the Eucharist. The heavenly grace conferred in the sacrament cannot be separated from the tangible things that are used to convey it. They are bound together.

Our Gifts, God's Gifts

In the Mass, the place where this movement is seen most clearly is the Preparation of the Altar at the beginning of the Liturgy of the Eucharist. The altar is spread with the cloth, and the vessels and the book are arranged—signs that speak of the meal and the solemn ritual which is about to unfold. At the same time, the baskets are passed through the pews. Making a financial offering is one way we express our participation in the liturgy and in the life of the Church. Giving in proportion to our means is a reflection of our commitment to our faith, to our community, and to the charitable work of the Church, all of which our gifts help to sustain.

> ◆ **Accept graciously, O Lord,**
> **we pray, the offerings of your peoples,**
> **that, renewed by confession**
> **of your name and by Baptism,**
> **they may attain unending happiness.**
> **Through Christ our Lord.**
>
> —*The Roman Missal*, Prayer over the Offerings for Monday within the Octave of Easter

After the altar is prepared and the collection is taken, members of the community bring forward the collection and the bread and wine for the Eucharist. The procession of gifts is profoundly meaningful. Though only simple things—money, bread, and wine—are brought forward, we are, in a symbolic sense, offering everything we have and everything we are. Even though we probably didn't bake the bread or harvest the grapes for the wine, we are part of the community's offering. Every time we see the gifts coming forward, they should remind us to offer to God all "the fruit of the earth and work of human hands"[10]—our very being, our accomplishments, our failures, all we have made, done, and hoped for. It is not just bread, but ourselves—our humanity—that are placed on the altar to await transformation. It is not just wine that is poured out, but our sufferings and those of the whole human family. This reality is reflected in the silent prayer the priest prays just before the washing of his hands: "with humble spirit and contrite heart may *we* be accepted by you, O Lord, and may our sacrifice in your sight this day be pleasing to you, Lord God."[11] We are asking God to receive not only our gifts, but ourselves.

And God does receive what we offer. An ancient hymn for this part of the Mass highlights what is happening in this moment:

> Let all mortal flesh keep silence,
> And with fear and trembling stand;
> Ponder nothing earthly minded,
> For with blessing in his hand,
> Christ our God to earth descending,
> Comes, our homage to demand.
>
> King of kings, yet born of Mary,
> As of old on earth he stood,
> Lord of lords, in human vesture,
> In the Body and the Blood;
> He will give to all the faithful
> His own self for heav'nly food.[12]

The words of the hymn, which are based on a prayer reaching back to the sixth century, capture the mystery of this time of offering. We place bread and wine, "the work of human hands,"[13] on the altar, but we know that this is about Christ's work, not ours. This is an incarnational moment: just as Christ was "born of Mary" to walk the earth in the first Incarnation, so now he descends again to become "heav'nly food." The Eucharist is always about the Paschal Mystery, the Easter mystery of the passion, death, and Resurrection of Christ. But, in another sense, the Eucharist is also a Christmas mystery, because Christ becomes truly incarnate in the Eucharist, transforming bread and wine into his own Body and Blood. A prayer from the Mass makes this clear: "May the Holy Spirit, O Lord, / sanctify these gifts laid upon your altar, / just as he filled with his power the womb of the Blessed Virgin Mary."[14] It is the same Spirit, and the same Christ who comes to us in every Mass. As we place our gifts on the altar, Christ comes to meet us there.

Water and Wine

After the priest receives the gifts and comes to the altar, he holds the bread in his hands and thanks God for his goodness. Then he fills the chalice with wine. Before he gives thanks for the wine, however, he adds a little water to it. It's a brief moment, easy to miss, but full of meaning. This watering of the wine goes back to ancient times, when wine was quite thick and water was added to make it more drinkable. But the gesture has been retained in the Mass to this day because of its symbolic meaning. As the priest adds the water, he says quietly, "By the mystery of this water and wine, / may we come to share in the divinity of Christ, / who humbled himself to share our humanity."[15] The wine represents Christ; the water represents us. Once it is added to the wine, the water is inseparable from the wine. In a sense, it *is* wine now. In the same way, we who participate in the Eucharist become the Body of Christ, part of him. We cannot be separated from Christ, any more than Is the water can be taken back out of the wine. It is the perfect image of the "marvelous exchange" of the liturgy.

Praying with the Communion of Saints

When we celebrate the liturgy, especially the Mass, we are not alone. Through the Communion of Saints we are united with all believers. This communion embraces the living and the dead, those on earth and those in heaven. There are not two Churches—one on earth, one in heaven. The liturgy is not divided into two. There is one Church, one liturgy, and heaven and earth share in them together. This passage in Eucharistic Prayer I, the Roman Canon, reminds of this with wonderful imagery:

> In humble prayer we ask you, almighty God:
> command that these gifts be borne
> by the hands of your holy Angel
> to your altar on high
> in the sight of your divine majesty,

so that all of us, who through this participation at the altar
receive the most holy Body and Blood of your Son,
may be filled with every grace and heavenly blessing.

> ◆ **We are surrounded
> by so great a cloud
> of witnesses.**
>
> —Hebrews 12:1

The same gifts that we have placed upon
the altar are taken to "the altar on high," in
heaven. There is one altar, one worship in
which earth and heaven join. The liturgy we
celebrate on earth is also unfolding in
heaven. The Mass is where we are most
united with those who have gone before us.

Praying with the Heavenly Hosts

The Eucharistic Prayer begins with a dialogue ("Lift up your hearts")
and continues with the Preface. We typically think of a preface as the
part you can skip at the beginning of a book. In the Mass, the Preface is
a prayer of praise and thanksgiving for the work of God which the priest
says just before we sing the Holy, Holy, Holy. It varies with the feasts
and seasons of the liturgical year. In Advent, the Preface praises the God
who comes to us in Jesus and who will come again at the end of time. In
Easter, the Preface praises Christ who has risen and given us a share in
eternal life. The Prefaces are wonderfully varied—in fact, more than
fifty can be used for the celebration of the Mass.

The Preface always ends with words that point to the union of
heaven and earth in the liturgy which lead us toward the singing of the
Holy, Holy, Holy:

> And so, with the Angels and Archangels,
> and with the great multitude of the Saints,
> we sing the hymn of your praise,
> as without end we acclaim . . . [16]

The text varies, but the point is always the same: when we celebrate the Mass, we do not just imitate an image of heavenly worship.
We actually pray with the angels and saints, joining—for a moment—
in their unending hymn and uniting our voices with theirs.

Earth and heaven unite at the altar: "Holy, Holy, Holy Lord God of hosts. / Heaven and earth are full of your glory."[17] The first part of this prayer is based on Isaiah 6:2–3, the prophet's vision of heaven as a great Temple, where God is seated upon his throne and angels, stationed above, cry out "Holy, holy, holy is the LORD of hosts! / All the earth is filled with his glory!" From at least the fifth century onward, the Catholic liturgy has incorporated this prayer, but always with the added reference to heaven. Both earth *and* heaven are full of God's glory, and thus, in God, the separation between these seeming opposites can break down. The "marvelous exchange" is palpable as our prayer reaches to heaven while grace pours out upon us through the sacraments.

◆ **Seraphim were stationed above; each of them had six wings: with two they covered their faces, with two they covered their feet, and with two they hovered.**

One cried out to the other:

"Holy, holy, holy is the LORD of hosts!

All the earth is filled with his glory!"

—Isaiah 6:2–3

The Liturgy and the Trinity

In the liturgy, we honor the Triune God. Christ is the center of our worship, and Christ is the high priest who presides at every liturgy—through the priest in the person of Christ, the head, and through us, as members of the Body of Christ. But the God we worship is both one and three—a Triune God, Father, Son, and Holy Spirit—and the liturgy is the action of the entire Trinity. Every liturgy begins by calling upon the Triune God: "In the name of the Father, and of the Son, and of the Holy Spirit." In the Eucharist, we pray to God the Father, through Christ, in the power of the Holy Spirit. The Eucharistic Prayer is the place where the Trinitarian nature of the liturgy is most clearly seen.

Thanksgiving to God the Father

The Eucharistic Prayer is a prayer of thanksgiving to God the Father. The very word *Eucharist* means "thanksgiving." At the beginning of the Liturgy of the Eucharist, the priest invites us into the prayer with the words "Let us give thanks to the Lord our God," to which the assembly responds, "It is right and just." Each of the Eucharistic Prayers (there are ten different forms of this prayer) is a prayer of thanksgiving to God the Father. The beginning of Eucharistic Prayer III expresses why we thank God:

> You are indeed Holy, O Lord,
> and all you have created
> rightly gives you praise,
> for through your Son, our Lord Jesus Christ,
> by the power and working of the Holy Spirit,
> you give life to all things and make them holy,
> and you never cease to gather a people to yourself,
> so that from the rising of the sun to its setting
> a pure sacrifice may be offered to your name.

What do we thank God for? Everything! We join all of creation in praising God who gives life and holiness, who gathers a community of praise and gives us this "pure sacrifice" to be offered. Everything God gives us is given through Christ and in the Spirit: our life, our being, our worship flow from the action of the Triune God. Our worship itself is a gift of God, a sign of God's love for and favor to humanity.

Memorial of God the Son

The Eucharistic Prayer is a prayer of thanksgiving to God for his loving action in the world. Within this great prayer of thanksgiving, we obey Christ's command to "do this in remembrance of me."[18] Thus, the liturgy is a *memorial* sacrifice, a solemn remembering. After giving thanks to God in the first part of the Eucharistic Prayer, we move into the Institution Narrative, recalling what Christ did at the Last

Supper. This portion of the prayer is called the *anamnesis*, a Greek word that means "remembering."

Of course, this kind of remembering is more than a simple calling to mind. The Eucharist is not merely a mental activity, in which we think for a certain space of time about what Christ did for us. This remembering is embodied: it is enacted. The Eucharist is both thanksgiving and memorial. Even as we remember what Christ did long ago, Christ is truly present on the altar in the sacrament. Liturgical memory remembers the past but has the power to change the present. Pope Francis writes:

> This is why the Eucharistic commemoration does us so much good: it is not an abstract, cold and superficial memory, but a living remembrance that comforts us with God's love. A memory that is both recollection and imitation.[19]

As we celebrate the Eucharist, we remember the past, but something happens in the present. As we recall what Christ did at the Last Supper, we taste the bread and drink the cup just as his disciples did. We hear his words and we touch his Body in the Eucharist. The Mass recalls what Christ did but opens our eyes to what Christ *does*: Christ is active in the world, in the liturgy, and in each of our lives.

> ◆ How holy is this feast in which Christ is our food; his passion is recalled; grace fills our hearts; and we receive a pledge of the glory to come, alleluia.
>
> —St. Thomas Aquinas, *O sacrum convivium*

Through God the Holy Spirit

The Holy Spirit is ever-present when we celebrate the liturgy. The Spirit, dwelling in us, gives us the faith to come to the altar with our offering; and the Spirit's power makes Christ present in the offering. In this way, "the liturgy becomes the common work of the Holy Spirit and the Church."[20] The Mass is a joint effort—God the Holy Spirit, and us!

It is easy to overlook the action of the Holy Spirit in the liturgy, because most of the prayers of the Mass are addressed to God the

Father, and of course we receive the Risen Body of God the Son in the Eucharist. But nothing happens at Mass except through the working of the Spirit.

The Spirit's presence is most powerfully experienced during the epiclesis of the Eucharistic Prayer. *Epiclesis* is a Greek word that means "invocation" or "calling down from on high." In the Mass, the epiclesis happens when the celebrant extends his hands over the bread and wine before the consecration. This ancient ritual gesture signifies the handing on of the Holy Spirit—it is the same gesture used when the bishop ordains or confirms, extending his hands over the individual or placing them on the head. It is the same gesture Christ used when he laid his hands on people to heal or bless. In the Mass, the priest calls the Holy Spirit down upon the gifts of bread and wine to transform them into the Body and Blood of Christ.

Eucharistic Prayer II gives us a glimpse of the mysterious way the Spirit acts in the liturgy: "Make holy, therefore, these gifts, we pray, / by sending down your Spirit upon them like the dewfall."[21] Just as the dew quietly appears on the earth overnight, so the Holy Spirit acts, unseen yet powerful, in the liturgy.

◆ **Come, Holy Spirit, come!**

And from your celestial home

Shed a ray of light divine!

—*Lectionary for Mass*, Sequence for Pentecost

After the consecration, the Holy Spirit is called down again in what is sometimes called the "second epiclesis." This time, the celebrant asks the Holy Spirit to come upon the Church. "Humbly we pray that, / partaking of the Body and Blood of Christ, / we may be gathered into one by the Holy Spirit."[22] The same Spirit who transforms the bread and wine into the Body and Blood of Christ is now called down upon all of us, to make us one and form us into the Body of Christ, capable of taking action in the world.

The Holy Spirit has many names: Comforter, Advocate, fire, finger of God's right hand. In the liturgy, through the Holy Spirit, the hand of God reaches out to touch us.

The Way of Beauty

We all know that beauty is subjective. What strikes one person as beautiful may not seem beautiful to another, and standards of beauty, whether in art or in the human form and face, vary from culture to culture. But when we talk about the beauty of the liturgy, we are talking about something much deeper than my taste, which

Christ . . . *is* beauty. ❖

may be different from yours. Pope Benedict XVI has written: "in Jesus we contemplate beauty and splendor at their source. This is no mere aestheticism, but the concrete way in which the truth of God's love in Christ encounters us, attracts us and delights us."[23] Christ is not simply beautiful; he *is* beauty.

The beauty of Christ lies beneath the surface. Indeed, in Holy Week we meditate on the words of Isaiah, "He had no majestic bearing to catch our eye, / no beauty to draw us to him,"[24] and we come forward one by one to contemplate his Cross. The image of the cross is so familiar to us that we can lose touch with the fact that it was an instrument of torture; only Christ's love had the power to transform an image of terror, pain, and punishment into a sign of salvation. In Christ crucified, we contemplate the deep beauty of God, who brings forth life out of death, and light out of darkness.

Thus, the Church speaks of the way of beauty. Since God is beautiful, Pope Francis writes, "every expression of true beauty can thus be acknowledged as a path leading to an encounter with the Lord Jesus."[25] Whatever is truly beautiful can lead us to God, because God made us to love what is beautiful. Beauty touches our hearts and attracts us. God made us that way!

Beauty is one of the ways God comes to meet us in the liturgy. And since beauty is an attribute of Christ himself, beauty is not an add-on, but "an essential element of the liturgical action."[26] The beauty of the liturgy in music, art, movement, and ritual is one of the ways the Church reflects the beauty of God. This beauty, like the beauty of Christ, is not limited to mere aesthetics, to my taste or your taste.

The way of beauty has still another dimension. Pope Francis has written, "evangelization with joy becomes beauty in the liturgy."[27] A community that does not evangelize, a community that lacks joy, cannot reflect the beauty of God, no matter how externally beautiful their church building might be, or how flawless the music, or how perfect the liturgy. A truly beautiful liturgy flows from a joyful community that is sharing the Gospel; in other words, true beauty always flows from Christ, who is God made visible.

❖ Questions for Discussion and Reflection

1. Read the prologue from the Gospel according to John (John 1:1–18). Why is the Incarnation so important?

2. How is the liturgy the work of the Trinity?

3. How do we collaborate with God in the liturgy?

4. How do we join in heavenly worship during the Mass?

5. What events in your life do you reflect on and remember every day? How do these events continue to change and influence you? How does our liturgical remembering change and influence us as Christians and as a Church?

6. Think of a time when a work of art—whether music, art, architecture, dance, sculpture—helped you draw closer to God. How did the art help you walk the "way of beauty" towards God?

Chapter 4
Liturgy Is a School of Faith

A WOMAN POINTS TOWARD THE ALTAR AS THE two young children at her side listen and wonder. She seems to be pointing the way to the mountaintop, explaining to the children what is happening. The art of Lalo Garcia reminds us that liturgy is not something we do all alone. Each of us, no matter who we are, needs guides along the way: parents or grandparents, pastors or teachers. Each of us has had many guides in coming to understand what it is we participate in when we celebrate the liturgy. Chances are we have been guides for others, whether we realize it or not.

And the liturgy itself is a teacher! When we think about religious education, we probably think of Sunday school catechists and Catholic school teachers. Maybe we think of bishops and priests, who are called to be the chief teachers in the Catholic community. But do we think of the liturgy as part of our formation in faith?

In the *Constitution on the Sacred Liturgy*, the bishops of the Second Vatican Council speak of the power of the liturgy to form us: "Although the liturgy is above all things the worship of the divine majesty, it likewise contains rich instruction for the faithful."[1] In fact, the liturgy is the privileged place where the Holy Spirit "remind[s] you of all that [I] told you."[2] Listening to Christ's Word, and sharing the Eucharist in his memory, we encounter the divine presence, and we continue to be formed as disciples of Christ. And since our participation in the liturgy is not a one-time event, but part of the weekly or even daily rhythm of our lives, we never cease to be disciples: the learning goes on and on.

Liturgy is, of course, not a classroom, and its primary purpose is not to educate. But the liturgy surely forms us. As we pray the liturgy and participate in the liturgy, what we believe is gradually shaped by the liturgy. "Good celebrations can foster and nourish faith. Poor celebrations may weaken it."[3] That is why the way we celebrate the liturgy is so important: the words we use, the songs we sing, the way we gather, how we participate—all of these directly impact our life of faith.

Lex Orandi, Lex Credendi, Lex Vivendi

The Latin phrase *lex orandi, lex credendi* goes back to the fifth century and is attributed to Prosper of Aquitaine, a fifth century Christian writer. Literally translated "law of prayer, law of belief," the phrase expresses the relationship between liturgy and faith. The "law of prayer"—the liturgy—establishes and shapes "the law of belief"—the teaching of the Church. In other words, how we pray both expresses and influences what we believe as Catholics. In more recent years, a third dimension has been added to this: *lex orandi, lex credendi, lex vivendi.* The dynamic of faith and prayer must in turn shape how we live.

In the *Constitution on the Sacred Liturgy*, the bishops of the Second Vatican Council drew on many sources: the Scriptures, the writings of the Fathers and Doctors of the early Church, and the decrees of the Council of Trent (1545–1563) which followed the Protestant Reformation. But eight different times, the authority cited for the Church's teaching on the liturgy comes from the liturgy itself. The bishops of the Council quoted prayers from the Mass and the Liturgy of the Hours. Along with the Scriptures, the prayers of the liturgy are a treasury of faith, a source of sound theology. Pope Benedict XVI wrote of the the great "riches" to be found in the Missal and in the Lectionary: "These texts contain riches which have preserved and expressed the faith and experience of the People of God over its two-thousand-year history."[4] The liturgy is a treasury where the Church has gathered the prayers and texts that express what we believe and who we are.

> Sometimes the way we pray is changed to reflect more clearly what we believe. ❖

The movement is not all in one direction, however. There has always been a back-and-forth between Catholic teaching and Catholic worship. Sometimes the way we pray is changed to reflect more clearly what we believe. The reform of the liturgy after the Second Vatican Council is a prime example of that. Since the Council, more changes— some hardly noticeable, some, like the revised translation of the prayers of the Mass in 2011, more so—have come our way, always with the intent of allowing the liturgy to express more clearly what we believe about Christ's presence and action in the world.

And since Catholic theology evolves, the liturgy evolves, too. Several newer liturgical rites and prayers reflect a growing awareness of the need to reverence human life right from the womb. The United States bishops recently published a special blessing prayer for a child in the womb, the first time we have had an official prayer of this kind. There are also Mass prayers for giving thanks to God for the gift of human life. The liturgy is in harmony with what we believe.

Most of us would probably expect that Church teaching would influence the prayers we say. Does it surprise you that it can go both ways—and that prayers can influence what we believe? This pattern is actually quite an ancient one. In both the Old and New Testaments, some of the oldest texts are liturgical songs. Think of Miriam's song after the crossing of the Red Sea in Exodus 15, which is thought to be one of the earliest passages in the Old Testament. In the New Testament, it is much the same. Both St. Paul and St. Peter quote hymn texts that would have been familiar to their readers and listeners and use them to emphasize or illustrate their teaching about the faith (take a look at Philippians 2:6–11, Colossians 1:15–20, or 2 Timothy 2:11–13).

> Prayer shapes belief and belief shapes life. ❖

Although we may not realize it, we probably do the same when we are asked questions about our faith. When asked about the role of Mary in the Church, most of us can't cite passages from the *Catechism of the Catholic Church* or from the documents of the Second Vatican Council on Mary. But we can certainly turn to traditional prayers like the Hail Mary and find good answers there. When we are asked about prayer, we can look to the Our Father. Liturgical prayer, with its deep roots in the Scriptures, has already formed what we understand about our faith whether we realize it or not.

Lex orandi, lex credendi, lex vivendi. Prayer shapes belief and belief shapes life. If our worship and our faith do not impact how we live, then they are meaningless. If our shared worship is truly a source, a fount, then it should not just seep out the edges of our lives, but flow abundantly, touching and changing everything. This is the hard part: we are asked to find Christ not in the serene beauty of shared prayer, but in the messy circumstances of our families and relationships, our communities, our nation, and our world. We will reflect more on this call to bring the liturgy to life in the last chapter.

School of Prayer

In addition to revealing the faith to us, the Mass forms us in *how* to pray. The Mass is one great prayer, in which we join in Christ's prayer to the Father. The Church speaks about five forms of prayer: blessing and adoration, petition, intercession, thanksgiving, and praise. The Mass encompasses all of these. As we celebrate the liturgy, we learn to pray as the Church prays.

Blessing and Adoration

"We bless you. We adore you," we pray in the Gloria. How can we bless God? Because blessing is an "encounter between God and [humanity],"[5] and encounters take two. Thus, blessings go both ways: we bless God in response to the blessings God has given us. Because God has blessed us with faith, we are able to acknowledge and bless God as the very source of blessing. As we explored in chapter 3, the Mass is a place of encounter with God, a divine exchange between heaven and earth— a mutual blessing. "From the liturgy . . . particularly the eucharist, grace is poured forth upon us as from a fountain."[6] Our response to this outpouring of grace is to bless and adore God.

Petition

Prayer of petition comes from humility, from an awareness that we are creatures, not creators. Knowing who

◆ **Lord, teach us to pray.**
—Luke 11:1

we are helps us to recognize who God is and to desire a relationship with God.[7] Petition starts with a desire for God's forgiveness, and looks towards the coming of the Kingdom. In the Mass, the Penitential Act is a prayer of petition: "Lord, have mercy. Christ, have mercy. Lord, have mercy." We acknowledge our weakness and we ask for God's mercy. Prayer of petition is prayer of conversion, in the sense that it is a turning away from self and toward God.

The Penitential Act is not the only example of petition in the Mass. We come back to this place of humility in God's presence over and over. As we bring bread and wine to the altar, we know that it is God's power, and not our own, that will transform them. And just before receiving Holy Communion we pray, "Lord, I am not worthy / that you should enter under my roof, / but only say the word / and my soul shall be healed."

Intercession

Intercessory prayer flows out of petition. Intercessory prayer is when we pray to God on behalf of others. Intercession is the "characteristic of a heart attuned to God's mercy"[8]—aware of God's goodness and mercy, we do not hesitate to bring before God all the needs around us, great and small. In praying for others, even our enemies, we imitate Christ's own prayer.

In the Mass, there are two main places where we offer intercessory prayer. One is the Universal Prayer or the Prayer of the Faithful. These intercessions are supposed to be broad in their scope. They embrace the needs not only of the local community but of the whole Church; and not only of the Church but of the world and those in affliction. When we offer the Universal Prayer or the Prayer of the Faithful, or whenever we offer intercessory prayers on behalf of others, we are exercising our own priesthood as members of the royal priesthood of the baptized. A priest is someone who intercedes with God on behalf of others, and in that sense, we are at our most priestly when we offer prayer of intercession.

> In praying for others, . . . we imitate Christ's own prayer. ❖

The second place in the Mass where we offer prayer of intercession is following the consecration in the Eucharistic Prayer. In this holy time, when Christ's Body and Blood is before us at the altar, we ask God to remember the living and the dead. We pray for unity, that through our sharing in the Eucharist "we may be gathered into one by the Holy Spirit."[9] We pray for the pope, the local bishop, and all the clergy. We pray for the "the peace and salvation of all the world"[10] and we ask that the Spirit might take "away everything / that estranges us from one another."[11] We pray for the dead "who have gone before us with the sign of faith."[12] And we pray for ourselves, that one day "we may come to an eternal dwelling place."[13] The breadth of the Church's intercessory prayer in the liturgy reminds us that the embrace of our personal prayer must be similarly wide.

Thanksgiving

In the liturgy, we thank God for everything. We thank God for his Word: our response to the Scripture readings is "thanks be to God." We thank God, above all, for Jesus Christ, and for every part of his life, his teaching, his death, and his Resurrection. Throughout the liturgical year, we thank God for what Christ has done and for what Christ continues to do. At Christmas Time, we thank God for the Incarnation, for being made visible among us in Christ. During Lent, we thank God for the gift of Lent itself, a time set apart for fasting, prayer, and works of mercy. At Easter Time, we thank God for restoring order to creation and raising up the universe in Christ's Resurrection. At the beginning of the Liturgy of the Eucharist, we pray: "Let us give thanks to the Lord our God." "It is right and just." And the very last words of the Mass are one last prayer of thanksgiving: "Go in peace." "Thanks be to God."

> The word "Eucharist" means "thanksgiving." ❖

Praise

"Praise is the form of prayer which recognizes most immediately that God is God. It lauds God for his own sake and gives him glory, quite beyond what he does, but simply because HE IS."[14] Prayer of praise flows from a pure heart, which no longer asks for anything, but simply loves God. The liturgy is full of praise language. Early in the Mass, we sing the Gloria, which is a song of blessing, thanksgiving, and praise. The Gloria rises to a crescendo, ending with a litany of praise of God simply for being God: "you alone are the Holy One, you alone are the Lord, you alone are the Most High, Jesus Christ, with the Holy Spirit, in the glory of God the Father."

Every part of the Mass is prayer, and the Mass encompasses every form of prayer. In this, the greatest prayer the Church offers, we come to know who we are in our weakness, and who we are called to be through Christ. And we come to know something of who God is, too: almighty, glorious, powerful, and near at hand. The liturgy is a school of prayer.

Formed by the Word of God

As we have seen, the liturgy does not simply recall the mysteries of Christ; in the liturgical remembering of them, they are made mysteriously present, especially the central mystery of Christ's passion, death, Resurrection—the Paschal Mystery. The same is true of the Scripture readings. Though many of them speak of past events, they are not in the past. As they are proclaimed in our midst, they speak to us in the present moment, and they give us a glimpse of what is yet to come —the fulfillment of God's Kingdom: "God's word shows us what we should hope for with such a longing that in this changing world our hearts will be set on the place where our true joys lie."[15] In God's Word, the heart

> ◆ When the Sacred Scriptures are read in the Church, God himself speaks to his people, and Christ, present in his word, proclaims the Gospel.
>
> —General Instruction of the Roman Missal, 29

of the Good News is handed on to us, so that we in turn may hand it on to others. At the table of the Word, we grow in wisdom, as from the table of the Eucharist we grow in holiness.

Listening and Learning

The Liturgy of the Word is the most clearly "teaching" moment of any liturgy. We sit to listen to the Word of God, which is proclaimed to us and then opened up through the homily. The Church has tremendous faith in the power of the Liturgy of the Word to form us as Christians. This is especially clear in the process for preparing new Christians, which is called the Rite of Christian Initiation of Adults (or RCIA for short). Those preparing for Baptism are called "catechumens," a Greek word meaning "hearers." And what do they hear? The Word of God! The very first time the Church prays over the catechumens in what is called the Rite of Acceptance, they are presented with a Bible. Because they are not baptized, they cannot join the community in receiving the Eucharist. However, they receive Christ again and again at the table of the Word. They join the community for the Liturgy of the

Word and then, just before the Liturgy of the Eucharist begins, they are dismissed to discuss, reflect, and pray about the Word of God they have heard. The study of the Word of God is a key part of their formation as Christians, which can last for many months—even years. The Word is their nourishment as they prepare for the sacraments. This Word of God has the power to change both minds and hearts, to transform doubters into believers, "hearers" into disciples.

The Liturgy of the Word, like the Liturgy of the Eucharist, is not something we passively absorb, but something we actively engage with. Through the Scriptures, we hear Christ's teaching and we encounter the living Christ, for God is present here as in the Incarnation: "the words of God, expressed in human language, are in every way like human speech, just as the Word of the eternal Father, when he took on himself the weak flesh of human beings, became like them."[16] God's wisdom is embodied in the words of the Scriptures just as God's Word becomes incarnate in Jesus Christ. Do we hear Christ's voice in the readings? Do we reverence his presence in the Scriptures?

> ◆ Blessed are those who hear the word of God and observe it.
> —Luke 11:28

Liturgy: Embodied Faith

Liturgy is much more than words on a page. Liturgy expresses and embodies our faith. It is important to learn about our faith—to study our tradition and to learn about prayer. But when we celebrate the liturgy, we also learn by doing. It is the difference between studying dance and dancing, between theory and practice. When we celebrate the sacraments, we speak a new language, for the language of the liturgy is "woven from signs and symbols."[17] These signs, symbols, and images quietly form our faith.

From the moment we enter the church building, we are surrounded by imagery that reminds us of who we are and points us beyond ourselves. The church building is the visible representation of the Body of Christ, living and active in the community. It is a reminder of God, dwelling in our midst. The church building is also an image of the heavenly city, because in this place our worship is joined to the unending worship of heaven. There is no one answer to the question "what does a church look like?" Churches come in every architectural style, and in all sizes and shapes.

> The church building . . . is a reminder of God. ❖

But there are some common features. Church buildings are often aspirational, reaching towards the heavens, inviting the gaze upward. They play with light, one of the key symbols of the divine presence, especially in their use of windows. Bells, towers, and spires extend a visible and audible invitation to worship to the surrounding community.

The church building invites our interaction from the moment we enter. The first thing we encounter after passing through the doors is often water—whether the baptismal font, often placed near the main entrance, or a small stoup or vessel of holy water. We stop and make the Sign of the Cross, blessing ourselves with the water. This simple gesture of blessing is a baptismal reminder. Thus, every time we enter the church building, we are reminded of our entry into the sacramental life through Baptism: "By baptism all are plunged into the paschal mystery of Christ: they die with him, are buried with him, and rise with him; they receive the spirit of adoption . . . and thus become true adorers whom the Father seeks."[18] Baptism is both our entry into the life of Christ and our call to offer worship to God through the liturgy. Every time we gather for liturgy we are reminded of this when we take the holy water at the door.

The altar is the focal point of the church building, the center of worship. Every time we pass the altar, we bow, acknowledging not a thing, but a person: the Risen Christ, present in our midst. Its prominence speaks of the centrality of the sacrifice of Christ, which the altar represents. The altar is also the table for the sacred meal that we carry out in Christ's memory, and points us towards the centrality of the Eucharist in the Church and in our lives. When we gather around the altar, we are reminded that the crucified and Risen Lord must be at the center of our lives outside the church as well.

The tabernacle, prominently displayed in the church building, is a constant reminder of the sacramental presence of Christ in the Church. When we genuflect before the tabernacle, or pause there to kneel to pray, we acknowledge the presence of the same Christ who comes to us at the altar. Silent adoration of the Blessed Sacrament leads us deeper into the mystery that is so simple and yet so unfathomable: Christ is here. Christ is with us. And we are with him. A story is told of St. John Vianney, the patron saint of priests, who spent many hours in prayer before the tabernacle. When he was asked what he said to Jesus, he replied, "I don't say anything. I look at Jesus and he looks at me."

The ambo, the place for the proclamation of the Word of God, is usually located close to the altar. The Word of God is central to our worship. In fact, the Church never comes together to pray the liturgy without sharing the Scriptures. All our liturgical prayers are imbued with scriptural language, because over the centuries the Church has learned to pray from meditation on the Scriptures. We pay special honor to the *Book of the Gospels*: it is carried in procession, placed

> Liturgical prayers are imbued with scriptural language. ❖

on the altar. We stand to hear the Gospel; even with our bodies we say something about what we believe about the Gospel accounts, in which we hear the voice of Christ. We are expressing our belief that the Word is a living presence in our midst and has the power to transform us.

The images of saints and angels that surround us when we pray— whether in statues, icons, or in the decorative elements of the church itself—tell us that we are not orphans: we are surrounded by the Communion of Saints, and we can turn to the saints in our prayer, seeking their intercession for ourselves, our loved ones, and our world. The church building is first and foremost a place to celebrate the Eucharist; but it is also a spiritual home for all who come to worship. As such it reflects both the liturgical and the devotional life of the faithful. Beloved devotions like the Rosary, the Stations of the Cross, visits to Mary, flowers and candles, all find a home here. When we participate in these devotions, we express our belief in the Communion of Saints, and the intercessory power of the Mother of God and all God's servants.

And whether a church building is large or small, there is always a place for the people. The pews and chairs offer a silent invitation to participate, to find our place in the community of believers. They tell us there is room for us in the Church.

> Our active participation is one way we express the intentionality of our faith. ❖

As the liturgy unfolds, we are invited into a solemn rhythm of prayer into which we enter not only with hearts and minds, but with voices and bodies. We join in responses. We stand; we kneel; we process. Our active participation is one way we express the intentionality of our faith. Participating in the liturgy is never a private experience and rarely is it a secret one. It is a declaration of our faith in Christ, of our unity with the Church.

We do not leave our bodies behind at the door and enter a realm of pure spirit. Quite the contrary: we pray with our bodies and we engage all our senses in our worship. Pope Benedict XVI has written, "by its very nature the liturgy operates on different levels of communication which enable it to engage the whole human person."[19] There is imagery to fill our vision—art and architecture, processions and movement, and changing liturgical colors that help us to be more mindful of seasons and mysteries of Christ. Our ears are filled with the Word of God, proclaimed and broken open, and with the prayers that are spoken and sung. We touch the hands of others and the broken bread that is Christ's Body. There are even smells to take in, especially the incense that surrounds the altar and the assembly with fragrance, an image and reminder of how our prayers rise to heaven like incense. And we taste the Body and Blood of Christ. In celebrating the liturgy, both body and soul are engaged, and the Eucharist we receive is nourishment for both body and soul. When we celebrate the Eucharist, we have one foot on earth, and one in heaven.

Learning by Doing

In the secular world, we are accustomed to a pattern of learning, then doing. We go to school, we study hard, and then, finally, the day of graduation arrives, we receive a diploma, and we move on. This pattern gets repeated over and over: learning is left behind. Students get asked what they are going to do in the real world, as though what they have been doing is somehow unreal.

In the Church, the pattern is different. We learn and prepare for the sacraments, but the deepest learning comes after receiving them. The early Church called this kind of learning *mystagogy*, a Greek word that means "teaching the mysteries." The neophytes—those newly baptized—were not taught everything there was to know about Baptism, Confirmation, and Eucharist in advance. Instead, the deeper meaning of the mysteries into which they had been initiated were explained to them over time. In the world of the liturgy, there is no graduation day. Since we believe that the sacraments work a change in us, leaving an indelible mark, the mysteries we celebrate grow clearer and clearer in hindsight.

St. Cyril of Jerusalem, the fourth-century bishop and Doctor of the Church, taught in this way. Some of his preaching survives in a collection called the *Catechetical Lectures*. He wrote:

> I long ago desired, true-born and dearly beloved children of the Church, to discourse to you concerning these spiritual and heavenly Mysteries; but knowing well, that seeing is far more persuasive than hearing, I waited till this season; that finding you more open to the influence of my words from this your experience, I might take and lead you to the brighter and more fragrant meadow of this present paradise.[20]

St. Cyril did not wait until after their Baptism in order to keep them in suspense! He waited because he knew that only experience of the sacraments could open up the meaning of the sacraments for them.

This kind of mystagogical exploration is what every Christian is called to do. Faith is not static nor is it self-explanatory. It must be continually learned. Even as we participate in the Eucharist, we need to explore what it means to participate in the Eucharist. In the Church, the pattern is not *learn then do*, but *learn and do and learn and do*. Through our reflection on liturgy, our faith is gradually shaped and our experience of the liturgy deepens. Participating in the liturgy is not a thought process: it is an adventure that engages our whole being.

This pattern continues. Liturgy does not stop at the mind and heart, but shapes our actions, too. How we live must become an expression of what we believe and how we pray. In other words, the pattern of self-giving we witness in the liturgy must become the pattern of our own lives. We believe that liturgy changes our lives and the lives of others. That is what we will explore in the next chapter.

> ◆ The authentic sense of the Eucharist becomes the school of active love for our neighbor. The Eucharist educates us to this love in a deeper way: it shows us, in fact, what value each person, our brother or sister, has in God's eyes, if Christ offers Himself equally to each one, under the species of bread and wine.
>
> —*The Mystery and Worship of the Eucharist (Dominicae cenae)*, 6

❖ Questions for Discussion and Reflection

1. Have you ever felt the Holy Spirit's presence, reminding you of Jesus' teaching at a key moment in your life?

2. What is your favorite Scripture passage? Why?

3. Do you recognize yourself and your own life in the readings of the Mass?

4. What is your favorite place in your own parish church? Why? How does it speak to you?

5. How do you prepare for and reflect on the Sunday liturgy?

6. Think of an aha moment you had in which you came to a deeper understanding of the liturgy.

Chapter 5

Liturgy Sends Us on Mission

T HE PAINTING BY LALO GARCIA ON THE COVER OF
this book has a stillness about it. We see people standing quietly
around the altar, or kneeling down, absorbed in prayer and contempla-
tion. But looking more closely, it is full of dynamic movement. There are
people on the journey, people bringing offerings, people drinking from
the river, people teaching, people learning—and people running!

In the detail pictured above, we see two figures coming down the
mountain. They are in a hurry—the feet of the figure on the left barely

touch the ground; the figure on the right reaches out eagerly. They are not hurrying in separate directions; in fact, their hands are joined—they are doing this together. A ray of light follows them and lights their path. Clearly, these two are not simply leaving the mountain; they are on a mission. They bring to mind the sending of Jesus' disciples: "He summoned the Twelve and began to send them out two by two."[1]

When we participate in the liturgy, we receive a mission: we are sent forth. This is not an optional part of the celebration. We cannot leave the mission to others while we remain at the altar or simply go about our business, perhaps returning to that busy city we see in the distance in Lalo Garcia's painting. Without the mission, the dynamic of the liturgy is incomplete. Through the prophet Isaiah, God said this in no uncertain terms:

> Your new moons and
>   festivals I detest;
> they weigh me down,
>   I tire of the load.
> When you spread out
>   your hands,
> I will close my eyes to you;
> Though you pray the more,
> I will not listen.
> Your hands are full of blood!
> Wash yourselves clean!
> Put away your misdeeds
>   from before my eyes;
> cease doing evil;
> learn to do good.
> Make justice your aim: redress the wronged,
> hear the orphan's plea, defend the widow.[2]

◆ [Jesus said:] "Well did Isaiah prophesy about you hypocrites, as it is written:

'This people honors me
   with their lips,
but their hearts are far
   from me;

In vain do they worship me,
teaching as doctrines
   human precepts.'"

—Mark 7:6–7

God harshly condemns religious practice that is divorced from action in the world. God tells the people not even to bother with ritual observances, feast days, and prayers while their "hands are full of blood." They have neglected the most vulnerable, the widow and the orphan;

they have ignored the cries of those in need. God turns away from the perfect liturgical observances of such people.

This powerful passage from Isaiah, which the Church proclaims each year during Lent, is a reminder that liturgy must never be divorced from service. Keeping the feasts and fasts, saying our prayers, and being in God's house Sunday after Sunday are all good things; but unless they overflow into action, they are meaningless. All too easily, we can put our religious practice in a box, thinking of it as a purely private matter between ourselves and God, and not letting it influence our relationships with other people or our engagement with the world around us. But that is not how this faith of ours works. We cannot become members of Christ's Body without also becoming members of *all* the members of Christ's Body. The very word "communion" reminds us that we are connected, not only with God but with each other. Pope Francis has said:

> ◆ **We should all ask ourselves before the Lord: How do I live the Eucharist?**
> —Pope Francis, Homily given on May 30, 2013

> The Eucharist is the sacrament of communion that brings us out of individualism so that we may follow him together, living out our faith in him. Therefore we should all ask ourselves before the Lord: how do I live the Eucharist? Do I live it anonymously or as a moment of true communion with the Lord, and also with all the brothers and sisters who share this same banquet?[3]

We talk of "receiving the Eucharist." But we must not stop there. As Pope Francis says, we need to "live the Eucharist." We cannot truly celebrate the liturgy, the memorial sacrifice of Christ's love, without loving those whom Christ loves: the poor and the afflicted, the outcast and the outsider.

The Church's liturgy pulls us in many directions. It draws us inward, toward a deeper communion with God and a fuller awareness of who we are, in our dignity and our weakness. It draws us upward towards communion with God and reminds us that this world is not our conclusion—we belong to the heavenly city. The liturgy also sends us outward. Liturgy gives us a mission. Liturgy that does not lead to action is incomplete, because mission is an integral part of the liturgy itself.

Liturgy: Inward and Outward

During the Second Vatican Council, a subtle change was made in the title of one of its documents. *Gaudium et spes,* the *Constitution on the Church **and** the Modern World,* became the *Constitution on the Church **in** the Modern World.* This slight modification spoke volumes. For centuries, the Church had seen herself as quite separate from the world: unchanging, uninfluenced, watching the world, a detached observer. That sense of a totally separate Church had never been quite true, however. The Church has changed over time, and has both influenced and been influenced by the ebb and flow of history. In changing "and" to "in," the Council Fathers were acknowledging the reality that the Church is indeed "in" the world, though not "of" the world.

That change from "and" to "in" expresses a tension which we encounter every time we celebrate the liturgy, the tension between the temporal and the eternal, the tension between the kingdom of this world and the Kingdom of God. This tension is not something to be eliminated or overcome. Rather, it is a fruitful tension that keeps us in a constant balancing act.

> The liturgy . . . calls us out of ourselves. ❖

The liturgy calls us into a sacred place, and a sacred time—God's time. The liturgy also calls us out of ourselves and our isolation into a community of people, with whom we are united and formed as the Body of Christ. Jesus invited his disciples to "come away by yourselves to a deserted place and rest a while."[4] The liturgy extends that same invitation to us.

But in entering into God's house and God's time, we do not abandon our problems and challenges in order to enter some imaginary world where there are no problems or challenges. That would be wishful thinking, not worship. Our problems and challenges come with us—our *world* comes with us when we celebrate the liturgy. Sometimes, we would like to build a wall between the world and the liturgy: "The Church should stay out of controversial issues." "I know there are problems in the world but I don't want to hear about them at Mass." "When I go to Mass I don't want to be made to feel uncomfortable." But shutting out the world only drains the liturgy of meaning, because our prayer is always directed towards the total transformation of our lives and of the world.

In the liturgy, God takes us in, changes us, and gives us back so that we can be instruments of transformation in our families and communities. Just as the bread and wine we offer are transformed and given back to us, we ourselves are changed and made new: we are given a charge to be missionary disciples, people who share and live the faith. The liturgy reminds us, again and again, that God is present not in some other world, but in this one; that Christ has offered himself on the cross not just for us, not just for some people, but for all people—those we love and those we find it hard to love, those who worship like we do and those who don't. The liturgy gives comfort; but it is not there to make us comfortable. Quite the reverse! The liturgy helps us to see the world as God does—filled with the divine presence and brimming with possibility. God invites us to become his coworkers. He opens our eyes to the sacredness around us, and invites us to participate in the divine project: healing what has become divided and broken, restoring creation to what God intended it to be.

> ◆ **All of the baptized are called to work toward the transformation of the world.**
>
> —*Co-Workers in the Vineyard of the Lord,* p. 8

Transforming Relationships

The liturgy transforms our relationships. That starts with our relationship with ourselves. In the liturgy, we acknowledge our weakness and God's strength. We recognize our frailty and sinfulness. At the same time, we are reminded, over and over, that this frailty and weakness has a destiny, a share in divine life. We are not alone. In the liturgy, we are still individuals but we are no longer isolated or lost. We have been found and drawn into a community with others. We are bound to others in the Body of Christ, called to act not only on our own, but as part of a community.

Once we recognize God's goodness to us, our relationships with others will start to be transformed. We will look at others as God looks at us: with love, gentleness, mercy, and forgiveness. How can we, as individuals and as a community, receive Christ who comes to us in the Eucharist and ignore the command of Christ? When he is asked which commandment is the most important, Jesus does not choose between earth and heaven. Instead, Jesus combines love of God and love of neighbor. Jesus puts love first and foremost, love that is not simply passive tolerance for the other, but embrace of the other.

> ◆ "You shall love the Lord your God with all your heart, with all your soul, with all your mind, and with all your strength." The second is this: "You shall love your neighbor as yourself." There is no other commandment greater than these.
>
> —Mark 12:30–31

In *God Is Love*, his document on Christian love, Pope Benedict XVI wrote about the great commandment of love and the Eucharist:

> I cannot possess Christ just for myself; I can belong to him only in union with all those who have become, or who will become, his own. Communion draws me out of myself towards him, and thus also towards unity with all Christians. We become "one body," completely joined in a single existence. Love of God and love of neighbor are now truly united.[5]

In the liturgy, intimate moments always open up to larger perspectives. "I confess to almighty God" is followed by "and to you, my brothers and sisters": sin is not just between me and God; it impacts the community. In the Eucharistic Prayer, the intimacy of the Institution Narrative is followed by a rapid widening of prayer, like ripples expanding in water, as we pray for those present and then for all the world. When we celebrate the liturgy, God is acting not only for those gathered but, in ways we can only begin to imagine, for the entire world, through us and beyond us. But in order to be part of that action of God in the world, we need to open ourselves up to transformation when we celebrate the liturgy.

The Liturgy Is Transformative

In this book we have explored the ways we encounter Christ in the liturgy. We have looked at the "marvelous exchange" that happens: Christ taking on our human life and giving us a share in divine life. We have seen the formative power of liturgy, our school of faith. To participate in the Eucharist is to participate in something powerful. We become what we receive, and what we receive is Christ's Body, broken on the cross, and his Blood, shed for the salvation of the world. Receiving the broken bread and drinking from the cup, we are challenged "to break ourselves . . . for others," in the words of Pope Francis.[6] Nothing more, and nothing less is asked of us than this: to do what Jesus did, to let our own lives be broken and poured out in service of others.

> The Eucharist can transform us in every way. ❖

Our participation in the Eucharist is incomplete if the Eucharist does not change us. In his prayer of preparation for Mass, St. Ambrose prayed that the Eucharist might take effect in his life, bringing forgiveness of sins, purity of conscience, and a new resolve to do God's work in the world. The saints know well that the Eucharist can transform us in every way—inside and out, body and soul—and that transformation leads to action.

During the Mass, the Prayers after Communion clearly express this desire for transformation. As the Mass comes to an end, we ask God for the fruits of the Eucharist: for the internal and external change our participation in this sacrament can bring.

What sort of transformation can the Eucharist work? There is no limit. Through us, the Eucharist can transform the world. The Eucharist can make us instruments of salvation and evangelizers. The Eucharist is good news for the poor. The Eucharist makes us messengers of peace and reconciliation. The Eucharist proclaims the Gospel of Jesus Christ to the nations. The Eucharist, the sacrament of unity, inspires our desire for unity. As Christians, we live with one foot always in eternity, yet we are to balance that longing for heaven with active engagement with the world.

The Eucharist is a mystery of self-sacrificing love. Every time we participate in it, every time we receive Communion, we acknowledge our own need for transformation, and we say yes to becoming instruments for the transformation God wants to bring to the world.

> ◆ We have partaken of the gifts of this sacred mystery, humbly imploring, O Lord, that what your Son commanded us to do in memory of him may bring us growth in charity.
>
> —*The Roman Missal*, Prayer after Communion for Saturday of the Second Week of Easter

The Dismissal: Let Out—or Sent?

Have you noticed how much of the Mass precedes Communion, and how little follows it? There is one more prayer, perhaps a hymn, a blessing, and the dismissal. The pattern of the Mass reflects that the Eucharist is not something to be hoarded and kept amongst ourselves: it is something to be shared outside the Church, and as quickly as possible!

The Mass ends with the dismissal. In fact, the word "Mass" comes from the last words the deacon or priest speaks at the Eucharistic liturgy: *Ite, missa est*, which can be translated "go, she is sent." At the end of Mass, we are not simply let out, as when the bell or buzzer goes off at the end of the school day. We are dismissed not to bide our time until we dutifully return the next Sunday. The word "Mass" has the same root as the word "mission." We are "sent" for a purpose, to be the Body of Christ in the world:

❖ Go forth, the Mass is ended.

❖ Go and announce the Gospel of the Lord.

❖ **Go in peace, glorifying the Lord by your life.**

❖ **Go in peace.**[7]

The formulas for dismissal reflect the mission we are given when we celebrate Mass. Eucharist is a call to go out, to evangelize, to glorify God by the way we live our lives, to be instruments of peace in the world.

Liturgy and Life

Recent popes have written extensively about the link between liturgy and life. In his letter for the Year of the Eucharist in 2002, St. Pope John Paul II wrote of the integral connection between liturgy and service: "We cannot delude ourselves: by our mutual love and, in particular, by our concern for those in need we will be recognized as true followers of Christ. . . . This will be the criterion by which the authenticity of our Eucharistic celebrations is judged."[8]

To celebrate the liturgy without expressing it in our lives through service of others is to omit something integral to the liturgy. If our proclamation of Christ remains within the walls of the Church, it is unfulfilled. Our active engagement in the liturgy needs to overflow in active engagement with the world. In the words of Pope Benedict XVI, "Eucharistic communion includes the reality both of being loved and of loving others in turn. A Eucharist which does not

> ◆ **For I was hungry and you gave me no food, I was thirsty and you gave me no drink, a stranger and you gave me no welcome, naked and you gave me no clothing, ill and in prison, and you did not care for me.**
>
> —Matthew 25:42–43

pass over into the concrete practice of love is intrinsically fragmented."[9] Pope Francis has written of the temptation religious people experience to stay safe, to remain within the walls of the Church, focusing on internal Church matters, including the liturgy itself. But this disconnect between liturgy and life is dangerous: "the mark of Christ, incarnate, crucified and risen, is not present."[10] In words that are now famous, Pope Francis says, "I prefer a Church which is bruised, hurting, and dirty because it has been out on the streets, rather than a Church which is unhealthy from being confined and from clinging to its own security."[11] There is no debate about it: liturgy and service are interdependent.

Liturgy comes to life when we allow ourselves to be broken open in compassion for refugees, migrants, and immigrants, struggling for survival or seeking safety and a better life for their families. Liturgy comes to life when we go forth to encounter the other—those of different races, creeds, or ways of life—and recognize them as beloved children of God. Liturgy comes to life when we take up our responsibility as citizens, advocating for the unborn, for prisoners on death row, for life at every stage. Liturgy comes to life when the self-giving love of Christ impacts the way we engage with other people in our daily lives, in person and on social media. Liturgy comes to life when we let the pattern of Christ's life become the pattern of our own lives.

> ◆ The Eucharist propels us
> forth to transform the world.
> —*Sacraments and Social Mission:*
> *Living the Gospel, Being Disciples*, 13

The Liturgy Is the Source and Summit of Our Faith

In this book, we have reflected on these key words from the *Constitution on the Sacred Liturgy* of the Second Vatican Council:

> The liturgy is the *summit* toward which the activity of the Church is directed; at the same time it is the *fount* [source] from which all the Church's power flows. For the aim and object of apostolic works is that all who are made children of God by faith and baptism should come together to praise God in the midst of his Church, to take part in the sacrifice, and to eat the Lord's Supper.[12]

In the liturgy, we are fed from the table of the Word and the table of the Eucharist so that we can have the strength we need to carry out

Christ's work in the world. As a Church, we work to provide things that are fundamental to living with dignity—food, shelter, health care, consolation, education, companionship, justice, peace. We do this because we recognize Christ in every human person, especially those who are poor or afflicted in any way. Our service proclaims the One in whom we believe, and thus serving the poor is a profession of faith which parallels and reinforces the recitation of the Creed at Mass.

The world watches Christians. Even those who do not believe as we do know the core of Christ's teaching—"love your neighbor as yourself."[13] The world today is as hungry to see Christ as were the people who crowded around to listen to him and be healed by him two thousand years ago. Today, we are Christ's Body in the world. Our actions can either reveal his presence and show people what Christ is like or obscure him.

The movement toward renewal of the liturgy that began in the late nineteenth century, gathered steam in the twentieth, and bore fruit with the reforms of the Second Vatican Council, had as its primary goal not simply the restoration of the liturgy to a more ancient form, or the introduction of the vernacular, or any of the other external aspects we might associate with the renewal of the liturgy. Rather, the drive towards liturgical renewal had as its primary goal the transformation of the world. Because how could people fail to be transformed if they understood what was happening in the liturgy? And if Catholics were transformed, how could the world not be changed for the good?

> ◆ True love is delicate and kind, full of gentle perception and understanding, full of beauty and grace, full of joy unutterable. There should be some flavor of this in all our love for others. We are all one. We are one flesh in the Mystical Body as man and woman are said to be one flesh in marriage. With such a love one would see all things new; we would begin to see people as they really are, as God sees them.
>
> —Dorothy Day, "On Pilgrimage"

So we come to the liturgy, to the source of grace and blessing, and we let ourselves be incorporated into Christ's Body. We accept the challenge to go forth to a world in need and act as Christ's Body, striving to reflect his self-sacrificing love, to share the Good News, and to serve others in his name. Then, we come back to the liturgy: we bring all we have done and all we have failed to do with us, and we climb once again to the summit of our Christian lives—the weekly Sunday Eucharist.

❖ Questions for Discussion and Reflection

1. How do you live the liturgy in your daily life? Do you live your faith outside of church or is there a gap there? What needs to happen to bridge that gap?

2. Have you ever experienced liturgy as "source"—where something you encountered in the liturgy became the source for living the Gospel more fully in your life?

3. Is the liturgy the "summit" of your Christian life? What hopes, dreams, successes, failures, and prayers do you bring with you to this summit?

NOTES

Introduction

1. Mark 6:31.
2. *Constitution on the Sacred Liturgy* (*Sacrosanctum concilium*), 10; emphasis added.
3. *Dogmatic Constitution on the Church* (*Lumen gentium*), 10; see also *Constitution on the Sacred Liturgy* (*Sacrosanctum concilium*), 10.

Chapter 1

1. *Constitution on the Sacred Liturgy* (*Sacrosanctum concilium*), 10.
2. Isaiah 2:2.
3. Emphasis was added to the biblical quotations.
4. Hebrews 8:1–2; emphasis added.
5. *Constitution on the Sacred Liturgy* (*Sacrosanctum concilium*), 7.
6. *Rite of Baptism for Children*, 62.
7. *Constitution on the Sacred Liturgy* (*Sacrosanctum concilium*), 7.
8. See Luke 18:1.
9. *Constitution on the Sacred Liturgy* (*Sacrosanctum concilium*), 2.
10. See Luke 4:16.
11. See John 7.
12. See Mark 14:1.
13. See Matthew 28:1.
14. Acts of the Apostles 2:46.
15. Acts of the Apostles 2:42.
16. Quoted in *The Liturgy of the Hours*, vol. 2 (New York: Catholic Book Publishing Corp., 1976), p. 695, Office of Readings for the Third Sunday of Easter.
17. See *Constitution on the Sacred Liturgy* (*Sacrosanctum concilium*), 2.
18. Acts of the Apostles 17:28.

Chapter 2

1. Luke 24:30–32.
2. 1 Corinthians 2:7.
3. 1 Timothy 3:16.
4. 1 Timothy 3:16.
5. 1 Corinthians 15:17, 19.
6. *The Roman Missal*, the Easter Proclamation (*Exsultet*) at the Easter Vigil.
7. Homily for the Easter Vigil, given April 15, 2006, accessed September 22, 2017, http://w2.vatican.va/content/benedict-xvi/en/homilies/2006/documents/hf_ben-xvi_hom_20060415_veglia-pasquale.html.

8. See *The Roman Missal*, Collect, Prayer over the Offerings, Preface, and Prayer after Communion for the Solemnity of the Most Holy Body and Blood of Christ (Corpus Christi).

9. *Stay with Us, Lord (Mane nobiscum Domine)*, 14.

10. *Lectionary for Mass*, Sequence for the Solemnity of the Most Holy Body and Blood of Christ (Corpus Christi).

11. John 6:55.

12. *Constitution on the Sacred Liturgy (Sacrosanctum concilium)*, 7.

13. See page XX.

14. *Constitution on the Sacred Liturgy (Sacrosanctum concilium)*, 51.

15. Luke 4:21.

16. Luke 24:27.

17. *Introduction to the Lectionary for Mass*, 5.

18. *Constitution on the Sacred Liturgy (Sacrosanctum concilium)*, 7.

19. *Constitution on the Sacred Liturgy (Sacrosanctum concilium)*, 7.

20. Matthew 14:15.

21. Matthew 14:16.

22. See Isaiah 25:6.

23. Quoted in *The Liturgy of the Hours*, vol. 3 (New York: Catholic Book Publishing Corp., 1975), p. 465, Office of Readings for Wednesday of the Fourteenth Week in Ordinary Time.

24. Revelation 7:9.

25. *Constitution on the Sacred Liturgy (Sacrosanctum concilium)*, 7.

26. *Constitution on the Sacred Liturgy (Sacrosanctum concilium)*, 33.

27. *Constitution on the Sacred Liturgy (Sacrosanctum concilium)*, 14; emphasis added.

28. *Sing to the Lord: Music in Divine Worship*, 14.

Chapter 3

1. See Ezekiel 47.

2. Revelation 22:1–3.

3. John 19:33–35.

4. *The Roman Missal*, Preface for the Solemnity of the Most Sacred Heart of Jesus.

5. Isaiah 12:3.

6. Gerard Manley Hopkins, "God's Grandeur," line 1.

7. *The Liturgy of the Hours*, antiphon 1, Evening Prayer I for the Solemnity of Mary, the Holy Mother of God.

8. Matthew 26:41.

9. *Constitution on the Sacred Liturgy (Sacrosanctum concilium)*, 2.

10. *The Roman Missal*, the Order of Mass.

11. *The Roman Missal*, the Order of Mass; emphasis added.

12. "Let All Mortal Flesh Keep Silence," translated by Gerald Moultrie.

13. *The Roman Missal*, the Order of Mass.

14. *The Roman Missal*, Prayer over the Offerings for the Fourth Sunday of Advent.

15. *The Roman Missal*, the Order of Mass.

16. *The Roman Missal*, Preface I of Saints.

17. *The Roman Missal*, the Order of Mass.

18. 1 Corinthians 11:24 and 25.

19. Homily for the Solemnity of the Body and Blood of Christ, given June 18, 2017, accessed September 27, 2017, w2.vatican.va/content/francesco/en/homilies/2017/documents/papa-francesco_20170618_omelia-corpus-domini.html.

20. *Catechism of the Catholic Church*, 1091.

21. *The Roman Missal*, Eucharistic Prayer II.

22. *The Roman Missal*, Eucharistic Prayer II.

23. *The Sacrament of Charity* (*Sacramentum caritatis*), 35.

24. Isaiah 53:2.

25. *The Joy of the Gospel* (*Evangelii gaudium*), 167.

26. *The Sacrament of Charity* (*Sacramentum caritatis*), 35.

27. *The Joy of the Gospel* (*Evangelii gaudium*), 24.

Chapter 4

1. *Constitution on the Sacred Liturgy* (*Sacrosanctum concilium*), 33.

2. John 14:26.

3. *Sing to the Lord: Music in Divine Worship*, 5.

4. *The Sacrament of Charity* (*Sacramentum caritatis*), 40.

5. *Catechism of the Catholic Church*, 2626.

6. *Constitution on the Sacred Liturgy* (*Sacrosanctum concilium*), 10.

7. See *Catechism of the Catholic Church*, 2629.

8. *Catechism of the Catholic Church*, 2635.

9. *The Roman Missal*, Eucharistic Prayer II.

10. *The Roman Missal*, Eucharistic Prayer III.

11. *The Roman Missal*, Eucharistic Prayer for Reconciliation II.

12. *The Roman Missal*, Eucharistic Prayer I.

13. *The Roman Missal*, Eucharistic Prayer for Use in Various Needs I–IV.

14. *Catechism of the Catholic Church*, 2639.

15. *Introduction to the Lectionary for Mass*, 7.

16. *The Dogmatic Constitution on Divine Revelation* (*Dei verbum*), 13.

17. *Catechism of the Catholic Church*, 1145.

18. *Constitution on the Sacred Liturgy* (*Sacrosanctum concilium*), 6.

19. *The Sacrament of Charity* (*Sacramentum caritatis*), 40.

20. Lecture 19.

Chapter 5

1. Mark 6:7.

2. Isaiah 1:14–17.

3. Homily for the Solemnity of the Most Holy Body and Blood of Christ (Corpus Christi), given May 30, 2013, accessed October 20, 2017, http://w2.vatican.va/content/francesco/en/homilies/2013/documents/papa-francesco_20130530_omelia-corpus-domini.html.

4. Mark 6:31.

5. *God Is Love (Deus caritas est)*, 14.

6. Homily for the Solemnity of the Most Holy Body and Blood of Christ (Corpus Christi), given on May 26, 2016, accessed October 20, 2017, http://w2.vatican.va/content/francesco/en/homilies/2016/documents/papa-francesco_20160526_omelia-corpus-domini.html.

7. *The Roman Missal*, the Order of Mass.

8. *Stay with Us, Lord (Mane nobiscum Domine)*, 28.

9. *God Is Love (Deus caritas est)*, 14.

10. *The Joy of the Gospel (Evangelii gaudium)*, 95.

11. *The Joy of the Gospel (Evangelii gaudium)*, 49.

12. *Constitution on the Sacred Liturgy (Sacrosanctum concilium)*, 10; emphasis added.

13. Mark 12:31.